ANNE McCAFFREY

Anne McCaffrey. Photograph by Greg Preston, Las Vegas, Nevada.

ANNE McCAFFREY

A Critical Companion

Robin Roberts

CRITICAL COMPANIONS TO POPULAR CONTEMPORARY WRITERS
Kathleen Gregory Klein, Series Editor

Greenwood Press
Westport, Connecticut • London

Library of Congress Cataloging-in-Publication Data

Roberts, Robin.
    Anne McCaffrey : a critical companion / Robin Roberts.
      p. cm.—(Critical companions to popular contemporary
writers, ISSN 1074–4193)
    Includes bibliographical references and index.
    ISBN 0–313–29450–X (alk. paper)
    1. McCaffrey, Anne—Criticism and interpretation. 2. Women and
literature—United States—History—20th century. 3. Women and
literature—Ireland—History—20th century. 4. Science fiction,
American—History and criticism. I. Title. II. Series.
PS3563.A255Z84   1996
813'.54—dc20   95–40029

British Library Cataloguing in Publication Data is available.

Library of Congress Catalog Card Number: 95–40029
ISBN: 0–313–29450–X
ISSN: 1074–4193

First published in 1996

Greenwood Press, 88 Post Road West, Westport, CT 06881
An imprint of Greenwood Publishing Group, Inc.

Printed in the United States of America

The paper used in this book complies with the
Permanent Paper Standard issued by the National
Information Standards Organization (Z39.48–1984).

10 9 8 7 6 5 4 3 2 1

To Jenny and Bryan Pisklo, Alison Roberts, Russell Roberts, Caitlin Cannon, Isabelle and Samuel Schexnayder, and Rosa Pulliam-Freedman, in the hope that the world that you grow up in is more like McCaffrey's vision of the future than the world we have today.

Contents

Series Foreword

The authors who appear in the series Critical Companions to Popular Contemporary Writers are all best-selling writers. They do not have only one successful novel, but a string of them. Fans, critics, and specialist readers eagerly anticipate their next book. For some, high cash advances and breakthrough sales figures are automatic; movie deals often follow. Some writers become household names, recognized by almost everyone.

But novels are read one by one. Each reader chooses to start and, more importantly, to finish a book because of what she or he finds there. The real test of a novel is in the satisfaction its readers experience. This series acknowledges the extraordinary involvement of readers and writers in creating a best-seller.

The authors included in this series were chosen by an Advisory Board composed of high school English teachers and high school and public librarians. They ranked a list of best-selling writers according to their popularity among different groups of readers. Writers in the top-ranked group who had not received book-length, academic literary analysis (or none in at least the past ten years) were chosen for the series. Because of this selection method, Critical Companions to Popular Contemporary Writers meets a need that is not addressed elsewhere.

The volumes in the series are written by scholars with particular expertise in analyzing popular fiction. These specialists add an academic focus on their best-selling writers to the popular success that these writers already enjoy.

The series is designed to appeal to a wide range of readers. The general reading public will find explanations for the appeal of these well-known writers. Fans will find biographical and fictional questions answered. Students will find literary analysis, discussions of fictional genres, carefully organized introductions to new ways of reading the novels, and bibliographies for additional research. Students will also be able to apply what they have learned from this book to their readings of future novels by these best-selling writers.

Each volume begins with a biographical chapter drawing on published information, autobiographies or memoirs, prior interviews, and, in some cases, interviews given especially for this series. A chapter on literary history and genres describes how the author's work fits into a larger literary context. The following chapters analyze the writer's most important, most popular, and most recent novels in detail. Each chapter focuses on a single novel. This approach, suggested by the Advisory Board as the most useful to student research, allows for an in-depth analysis of the writer's fiction. Close and careful readings with numerous examples show readers exactly how the novels work. These chapters are organized around three central elements: plot development (how the story line moves forward), character development (what the reader knows about the important figures), and theme (the significant ideas of the novel). Chapters may also include sections on generic conventions (how the novel is similar to or different from others in its same category of science fiction, fantasy, thriller, etc.), narrative point of view (who tells the story and how), symbols and literary language, and historical or social context. Each chapter ends with an "alternative reading" of the novel. The volume concludes with a primary and secondary bibliography, including reviews.

The Alternative Readings are a unique feature of this series. By demonstrating a particular way of reading each novel, they provide a clear example of how a specific perspective can reveal important aspects of the book. In each alternative reading section, one contemporary literary theory—such as feminist criticism, Marxism, new historicism, deconstruction, or Jungian psychological critique—is defined in brief, easily comprehensible language. That definition is then applied to the novel to highlight specific features that might go unnoticed or be understood differently in a more general reading of the novel. Each volume defines two or three specific theories, making them part of the reader's understanding of how diverse meanings may be constructed from a single novel.

Taken collectively, the volumes in the Critical Companions to Popular Contemporary Writers series provide a wide-ranging investigation of the complexities of current best-selling fiction. By treating these novels seriously as both literary works and publishing successes, the series demonstrates the potential of popular literature in contemporary culture.

Kathleen Gregory Klein
Southern Connecticut State University

Acknowledgments

I am grateful to Kathy Klein, who realized that Anne McCaffrey deserves more critical study, and to Barbara Rader and Nicole Burke, the editors at Greenwood Press. Carol Mattingly and Sharon Aronofsky Weltman provided invaluable suggestions for improvement and unceasing encouragement. To them I am especially indebted. Lucy, Tom, Bob C., and Darcy were very supportive, as were Peter Fischer, Emily Toth, Keith Kelleman, Rachel Kahn, Gayle, Linda and Shirley Roberts, Rosan Jordan, Frank de Caro, Pat Day, Carl Freedman, Susan Kohler, Kathie Gremillion, Laura and Harry Schexnayder. The students with whom I read Anne McCaffrey's works at the University of Pennsylvania, Lafayette College, Colby College, and Louisiana State University all contributed to this book. I owe Allison Mankin a special debt for introducing me to McCaffrey's work and encouraging me to teach it. Susan Bryson contributed her intelligence, energy, and efficiency to the secondary bibliography and index. Matthew Hargreaves' impressive bibliography was an inspiration and of great assistance. And, of course, we all owe a great deal to Anne McCaffrey, whose writings have provided pleasure and thought-provoking ideas to millions of grateful readers.

The Life of Anne McCaffrey

Anne McCaffrey's brief biographical statement in her novels is as intriguing as her fiction. In each novel appears a version of the following: "Between her frequent appearances in the United States and England as a lecturer and guest-of-honor at science-fiction conventions, Anne McCaffrey lives at Dragonhold, in the hills of County Wicklow, Ireland, with assorted horses, cats and a dog. Of herself, Ms. McCaffrey says: 'I have green eyes, silver hair, and freckles—the rest changes without notice.' "

This brief description suggests McCaffrey's lively sense of humor and interest in change. The name of her home refers to her most popular series, *The Dragonriders of Pern*. Born and raised in the United States, McCaffrey did not move to Ireland until she was in her thirties. While she is an Irish citizen now, she says, "Living in Ireland gives me a chance to feel slightly 'alien' " (E-mail 3-14-95). She also praises the way the Irish use language: "Language is used far more precisely in Ireland. That helps give flavor to dialogue" (E-mail 3-14-95).

The ability to create a believable alien and a believable sense of alienation in her characters can be traced to McCaffrey's early life and experiences. Her upbringing was shaped by her parents' encouragement and her sense of being different. In "Retrospection," she explains, "If I were asked to choose which influence was the most important in my life, I'd have to answer that it was parents. Neither fit the patterns of style

and behavior in the 1920s, '30s, and '40s for our middle-class status"
(20). She ascribes her parents' relative prosperity during the Depression
to her mother's premonition of the stock market disaster, which
prompted her parents to take their money out of the market. This mem-
orable intuition may be the source of McCaffrey's interest in telepathy
and precognition. Her mother was not able to go to college, but she took
college courses, was a copywriter, ad writer, wrote mysteries (that were
never published), became a real estate agent, and "supported herself
admirably after my father's death" (21). McCaffrey recounts her mother's
bravery during World War II, when she coped with her husband and
son being overseas, while another son was ill with osteomyelitis, an in-
flammation of the bone marrow. *Dragonquest* is dedicated to McCaffrey's
mother, Anne Dorothy McElroy McCaffrey. Of her mother's example,
McCaffrey writes, "Is it any wonder I write about strong women? From
early on, I was expected to achieve at a high level, constantly exhorted
to do so" ("Retrospection" 22).

Her father, George Herbert McCaffrey, PhD, was research director for
the Chamber of Commerce and Industry in New York City. An expert
in city planning and management, he wrote *Metropolitan Boston*. As a
Reserve Infantry lieutenant colonel, George McCaffrey was chief political
advisor to General Mark Clark, a military governor in Italy; there is a
bridge in Palermo named after him (Brizzi, *Anne McCaffrey* 4). He went
to Japan and helped the Japanese restructure their tax system and served
the United Nations Forces as "chief finance officer" ("Retrospection" 22).
The Ship Who Sang is dedicated to him. McCaffrey clearly admires both
of her "unorthodox parents, achieving in so many different occupations"
("Retrospection" 22).

Anne Inez McCaffrey was born on April 1, 1926. She had two brothers,
one older, Hugh, and one younger, Kevin. Hugh was a U.S. Army Major,
who died in 1987 and whose novel, *Khmer Gold*, was published posthu-
mously in 1988. Kevin was an insurance underwriter. McCaffrey's family
was quite literary; as Brizzi points out, "Anne McCaffrey's mother, father, older brother Hugh, and three nieces have all been writers, and her
son Todd has collaborated with her" (*Anne McCaffrey* 4). McCaffrey studied Slavonic languages and literature and graduated *cum laude* (with honors) from Radcliffe College in 1947. Even in college, she showed an
interest in science fiction; her honors thesis was entitled "Eugene Iva-
novich Zamiatan, With Special Emphasis on His Utopian Novel, *We*."
After graduation, she held a variety of jobs including advertising copywriter for Liberty Music Shops and cosmetics pioneer Helena Ruben-

stein. She also took voice lessons. In 1950 McCaffrey married Wright Johnson. They had three children: Alec in 1952, Todd in 1956, and Georgeanne in 1959. After a 1970 divorce, McCaffrey moved to Ireland with her two younger children and her mother.

Her experiences have left a mark on her fictions, for her own life did not follow a fairy tale plot. McCaffrey acknowledges that her fictions are radical revisions of the Cinderella story, in that "my heroines are victims who then show that they can survive whatever has victimized them. This is an important difference [from the Cinderella story] in both viewpoint and conclusion. It's certainly a different mindset . . . and very modern. Which is, I suppose, why my novels have appealed to women wishing to step out of traditional roles and into newer ones" (E-mail 3-9-95). She has also stepped out of a traditional role. McCaffrey describes her difficult situation quite matter-of-factly: "I was even, to my surprise, not only a battered wife (more psychologically than physically) but also a single parent since I took over the rearing of my children" (E-mail 3-9-95). To her parents, McCaffrey credits the inspiration that helped her. "I was also much sustained by a phrase that my parents would throw at me in their desperation to motivate me: 'Anne, you're going to go to college, marry, and have children: what are you going to do with the rest of your life?' " (E-mail 3-9-95).

McCaffrey also credits her interest in literature to her parents. Like many readers and writers, she had parents who read to her. Her parents' reading choices might seem unusual, and they certainly help explain why McCaffrey writes science fiction. Her father read her poetry by Kipling and Longfellow, and her mother selected Kipling's fiction and science fiction by A. Merrit. McCaffrey also identifies her love of literature with her sense of difference. She remembers herself as an "opinionated, asocial, extroverted, impossible egregious brat" ("Retrospection" 22) whose primary friends were books. She writes:

> The early lessons I learned, generally the hard way, in standing up for myself and my egocentricities, being proud of being 'different,' doing my own thing, gave me the strength of purpose to continue doing so later in life. You learn how not to conform, how to avoid labels. But it isn't easy! It's lonely until you realize that you have inner resources that those of the herd mentality cannot enjoy. That's where the mind learns the freedom to think science-fictiony things ("Retrospection" 23).

McCaffrey's experiences appear in the lives of many of her heroines and heroes, who similarly struggle through difficult times, often because of their difference from other people. However, like McCaffrey herself, her protagonists find happiness and success through perseverance. This plot helps explain the tremendous popularity of McCaffrey's fictions, for most adolescents and many adult readers have a similar sense of being out of step with the world. Her biography also provides hope for the outsider. As she writes, "No one, least of all me, suspected I'd spend [my life] writing science fiction. Or that such writing would be so popular and land me in a prestigious position within the field" (E-mail 3-9-95).

McCaffrey's interest and love of literature began early. She began writing at the age of eight, and "at Girl Scout camp, she wrote, produced, directed and starred in a fantasy-oriented play" (Brizzi, *Anne McCaffrey* 4). Brizzi notes that McCaffrey wrote a 20,000-word novel, *Eleutheria, the Dancing Slave*, in Latin class, and a western novel that focuses on horses, in junior high school.

Her lifelong interest in dramatics and music started early, and its influence can be seen in her fiction. McCaffrey studied voice for nine years and performed in or directed over thirty productions. Her roles included Queen Agravaine in *Once Upon a Mattress*, the Old Woman in *Candide*, Margot the Innkeeper in *The Vagabond King*, the Medium in Gian Carl Menotti's opera, *The Medium*, and roles in many other classic musicals such as *Kiss Me, Kate*, and light operas like *Die Fledermaus*. Of her voice, she writes, "Though I trained as a dramatic soprano and had both volume and range, like Killashandra [in *The Crystal Singer* series (see Chapter 5)], there was an unattractive burr in my voice, which was useful for singing character parts" rather than "the leads" ("Retrospection" 23). Her musical career was at its height from 1958 to 1965. "One of the musicians with whom she worked, Frederick N. Robinson of Pennsylvania's Lancaster Opera Workshop, became the model for Master Robinton, the kindly and visionary master musician of Pern" (Brizzi, *Anne McCaffrey* 5) (see Chapter 4). Not surprisingly, McCaffrey cites Master Robinton and Killashandra as two of her favorite characters (E-mail 4-22-95).

Soon after she was married, McCaffrey joined a local choir and other musical groups. There she studied with the choir master, and when she and her family moved to Germany, she studied with another trainer. Rod Stewart, her voice instructor, found the flaw in her voice, but her singing was so powerful that, as Matthew Hargreaves, her bibliographer, describes, "Anne could be heard over the full chorus, with the organ going full blast" (*Anne Inez McCaffrey, Forty Years* 4). McCaffrey's strength, determination, and skills were put to good use as stage director and performer. She considers her biggest musical and dramatic success to be her role as stage director and actress in the part of Alexa Hexa, a witch, in Carl Orff's *Ludus De Nato Infante Miricus* in its American premiere. Perhaps this experience explains why so many of her female protagonists are called "witch," lovingly and with admiration, by their lovers. Hargreaves says that McCaffrey quit the drama world when she became "fed up with the amateur personalities, temperaments, and backstage antics" (*Forty Years* 4). Drama's loss became the literary world's gain. McCaffrey clearly draws on these experiences with drama to depict headstrong and temperamental heroines such as Killashandra in *The Crystal Singer* series.

As do most writers, McCaffrey takes the facts and experiences of her life and transmutes them into art. All of McCaffrey's novels reveal her interest in family and children, and *The Ship Who Sang* and her realistic novels deal with divorce and related issues such as custody.

Perhaps because she made her fame and fortune writing science fiction, McCaffrey's "other" novels have been neglected by critics. Of these novels, McCaffrey writes, "I do such novels when the spirit, or the idea, move me to write them. I enjoyed doing these 'gothics' which were extremely popular in the late '60s and early '70s" (E-mail 4-12-95). These six novels, *Ring of Fear, The Mark of Merlin, The Kilternan Legacy, Stitch in Snow, The Year of the Lucy,* and *The Lady,* deserve study not only for what they reveal about McCaffrey's science fiction, but also as texts worthy of study themselves. Unfortunately, there is not space in this book to consider these texts fully. Because McCaffrey's science fiction is her most widely-read and most extensive work, this study focuses on the science fiction.

In her realistic novels, McCaffrey creates likeable young female heroines who narrate their tales of adventure and romance in the first person. But, as she does in her science fiction novels, McCaffrey creates original twists to conventional plots. McCaffrey can put only touches of her knowledge of the Irish and horses in her science fiction (such as the name Niall in *The Ship Who Sang,* for example), but the realistic novels draw directly on these experiences. She depicts unusual relationships between people and dragons in *The Dragonriders of Pern,* and in her realistic fiction she creates special and believable relationships between a woman and her dog (*The Mark of Merlin*), a woman and her horses and cat (*Ring of Fear*), a young girl and horses (*The Lady*).

Quoting a reader, McCaffrey approvingly says her non–science fiction books have been called "my 'people' stories because they ARE about people and not about someplace new or some new process" (E-mail 4-12-95). She further explains her heroines are "victims who became survivors. That's important for women today. To know that they can be down but don't have to be out" (E-mail 4-12-95). In *The Kilternan Legacy* and *The Lady*, McCaffrey raises important feminist issues, such as domestic violence, and exposes the inequitable treatment of women in the Irish legal system. In *The Year of the Lucy*, McCaffrey deals with domestic violence and the disintegration of a marriage, but she also focuses on the difficulties of being a woman artist. McCaffrey's "other" fiction, then, is remarkably similar in themes to her science fiction. But unlike science fiction, realistic fiction allows fewer optimistic surprises or innovations. Nevertheless, in the romance tradition of *Jane Eyre*, these novels do contain upbeat endings, with all the female characters happily finding mates. Just as *Jane Eyre* contains subversive feminist messages and a strong female character, so do McCaffrey's realistic novels. In a unique fashion, each of these novels challenges readers' ideas about relationships and gender. McCaffrey may draw on her own experiences in these realistic novels, but she transmutes the personal into art.

Her first publication provides an example of how McCaffrey draws upon and expands her own experiences to create powerful *science* fiction. While pregnant with her first son, Alec, McCaffrey developed the story idea that led to her first publication, "Freedom of the Race," in 1953 in the science fiction magazine, *Science Fiction Plus*. She wrote the story for a writing contest that called for a 1,000-word story with a surprise ending. The plot revolves around aliens who use human females as surrogate mothers for their own dying race. McCaffrey's pregnancy made her think about issues of reproduction, and by turning to science fiction, she extrapolated from her own experiences to create a thought-provoking fiction. Sam Moskowitz, a science fiction critic who was the editor at *Science Fiction Plus* at the time, praises the story's "solid detail about childbirth that gave the story an air of being based on science and real authenticity" (Hargreaves, *Anne Inez McCaffrey: Forty Years* 5). Another fascinating detail he provides is that it was Hugo Gernsback, the influential science fiction editor and publisher for whom the Hugo Award is named, who changed McCaffrey's original title for her first published story (from "The New Freedom"). Little did either of them know at the time that McCaffrey would become the first woman to win the Hugo Award, given annually by the World Science Fiction convention.

McCaffrey continued to write, but her fiction was not published with regularity. Her engaging and prescient or predictive story, "The Greatest Love," relates the story of a man's sister who acts as a surrogate mother long before *in vitro* fertilization was developed. Ironically, the story was not published until 1977; in the 1950s, the writer Judith Merril had described the story's events as "too far out" (Hargreaves, *Anne Inez McCaffrey: Forty Years* 7). While McCaffrey published her first short story in 1953, she did not begin to publish regularly until the 1960s, with the Helva stories that then turned into *The Ship Who Sang*. "The Ship Who Sang," the short story, gave McCaffrey her first important recognition in the science fiction world, and it was included in Judith Merril's collection of the best science fiction stories of 1962. Some of the other material that McCaffrey worked on at this time has since been reworked, and is part of the successful *Rowan Series* and *Doona Series* (see Chapters 6 and 9).

Like many writers, McCaffrey's writing career was not a linear progression, and with three small children to raise, and living in Germany with an unsupportive husband, she found it difficult to write. Hargreaves preserves Johnson's lack of approval by reproducing an article published about McCaffrey's first story: "Being a Princeton man, Mr. Johnson takes a somewhat dim view of his wife's flights into outer space" (6). The reporter's tone reveals a certain prejudice against women writers and science fiction. Hargreaves describes Johnson's wish that McCaffrey write more traditional high art, and characterizes his attitude as "a long-term schism between Anne and her husband" (8). However, McCaffrey does recount the encouragement she received from writer James Blish. Fortunately for her legions of readers, McCaffrey heeded Blish and her own instincts. In 1965, she turned to writing full-time, saving money for her children's college fund. In 1967 she published her first novel, *Restoree* (see Chapter 8), and "Weyr Search," her Hugo-Award winning story. McCaffrey was on her way to bestseller status, which she would achieve within a decade.

The first woman to win the Hugo, and the first woman to win the Nebula, the award given annually by the Science Fiction Writers of America Association, McCaffrey has received many other awards. In 1968, she won the Hugo for "Weyr Search" and the Nebula for "Dragon Rider," both of which became part of *Dragonflight*, the first novel in *The Dragonriders of Pern* series (see Chapters 3 and 4). *Dragonsong* won the

1976 Children's Book Showcase Award, the American Library Association Award for Notable Children's Books, and the 1977 Hornbook Fanfare Award. For *Dragonsinger* she received both the American Library Association Award for Notable Children's Books and their award for Best Books for Young Adults (in 1977). In 1979, *The White Dragon* received the Ditmar Award (Australia), the Gandalf Award, and the Streza Award (Eurocon, the European Science Fiction Convention). She has since won the genre's major awards and honors, including the E. E. Smith Memorial Award for Imaginative Fiction in 1976, and in 1980, the Balrog Award for Fantasy, Best Novel (*Dragondrums*), and Outstanding Achievement. McCaffrey was the first writer to receive The Science Fiction Book Club Award, and she continues to win it with regularity that she describes as "almost embarrassing" (E-mail 4-22-95). Most recently, she was Guest of Honor at the 1994 World Science Fiction Convention. Her works have sold over 17 million copies in the United States, Germany, and Japan. No figures are available for the other fourteen languages that her books have been translated into, so the actual total is much higher (E-mail 4-22-95).

From 1968 to 1970, McCaffrey served as secretary-treasurer of the Science Fiction Writers of America (SFWA). She writes that in this capacity, she "got to meet by writing or in person almost all the new writers and the established ones" (E-mail 3-14-95). She explains "I worked hard, and wrote very little, during those two years, but I also read everything that was printed in science fiction and fantasy" (E-mail 3-14-95). Such reading and professional involvement may provide the model for the association of Talents so important to *The Rowan* series. In those novels, a group of psychically gifted individuals band together to protect themselves and to better serve humanity. McCaffrey's work with SFWA may also have prepared her for her extensive support of and collaboration with other writers. Two of her books, *Alchemy and Academe* (1970), a collection of short stories edited by and with a foreword by McCaffrey, and *Cooking Out of This World* (1973), a collection of favorite recipes by science fiction writers and their spouses, demonstrate McCaffrey's interest in working with other writers. She is currently at work on another cookbook of recipes by science fiction writers.

A recent development in McCaffrey's writing career is her collaboration with younger, less established writers. McCaffrey has written books with Jody Lynn Nye, Elizabeth Moon, Elizabeth Ann Scarborough, Mercedes Lackey, and Steve Stirling. Modestly, McCaffrey praises the insights and contributions of her coauthors. For example, she praises

Moon's "competence and/or knowledge" (E-mail 3-9-95) and her improvement of a main character.

That McCaffrey herself is so popular a writer that her name and ideas are enough to sell books is another mark of her achievement as a writer. McCaffrey admires and acknowledges the influence of other writers, including Georgette Heyer, Andre Norton, Mercedes Lackey, Connie Willis, Dave Duncan, Robert Silverberg, and Gordon Dickson (E-mail 3-14-95). She praises Jane Yolen's *Briar Rose* and Elizabeth Ann Scarborough's *The Healer's War*, and also mentions Dick Francis, a mystery writer who writes about the world of horse racing, and Patricia Cornwall, Elizabeth Peters, Ellis Peters among others.

A flexible person, McCaffrey does not need a special place or atmosphere to do her writing. She says, "I can work anywhere, and have, so place is not important: the availability of a keyboard is. I prefer a quiet room and music but I have written in an air terminal and on an airplane" (E-mail 3-14-95). Her writing habits, then, are as a versatile as the prose she produces. She knows instinctually when it is time to move on to another series or book, and doesn't begin writing with a predetermined idea. "I'm finished with one series when I feel I don't have more to say within those parameters. . . . I need a circumstance, a conflict, or characters that need talking about to re-enter a series. So the story, or the characters themselves, always determine the focus" (E-mail 3-9-95).

McCaffrey's other interests include her animals, an interest that goes back to her childhood when she talked with the family cats. She enjoys knitting and sewing, although they are more difficult for her now because of her nearsightedness. Knitting plays an important part in *Stitch in Snow*, one of McCaffrey's realistic novels. She reads, cooks, and raises cats and Doberman puppies. McCaffrey and her daughter started a horse business in 1977, in which McCaffrey still participates when her writing and other demands permit. Dragonhold Stables has 14 stables on 47 acres, competition horses, and an indoor riding school. Readers interested in knowing more about McCaffrey's knowledge of horses will want to read *Ring of Fear* and *The Lady*.

This writer's sense of McCaffrey as a person, drawn from mail, E-mail correspondence, and published interviews, is that she is a modest and lively individual with a wonderful sense of humor, just the sort of person one would expect and hope to have written such engaging novels as those in *The Dragonriders of Pern* series.

2

The Genre of Science Fiction

THE SCIENCE FICTION WORLD

Science fiction is a broad category that is difficult to define because different writers and critics use the term to refer to a variety of approaches and texts. Perhaps the label's most common function is as a marketing device—science fiction readers look for it in a particular area of a bookstore. Mainstream writers like Margaret Atwood have written science fiction, but so have writers like Anne McCaffrey, who is known primarily for her genre writing.

Science fiction is unique in reader-fan relationships and sense of community. Special fan magazines, fanzines, connect science fiction readers and writers with criticism and reaction to science fiction of all types. Some fanzines specialize in the work of one author, others in types of science fiction. During the 1930s, 1940s, and 1950s especially, writers paid close attention to fan reaction to their works, and fans would frequently begin as readers and end up as writers. Isaac Asimov's career provides one example of this pattern. McCaffrey continues this pattern of appreciating her readers. Science fiction editors Greenberg and Gilliam describe McCaffrey autographing books for huge crowds, day after day, untiringly: "no wonder the loyalty of her fans is perhaps the strongest in the SF community" (Greenberg and Gilliam 32).

Science fiction readers and writers also interact at conventions, known as cons. In America, there are several cons each month, all over the country, which culminate in the annual World Science Fiction Convention. A con typically involves an art show based on science fiction themes and science fiction writers' work. In addition, cons usually have a book exhibit featuring rare science fiction books and magazines and also contemporary works. A costume show is the highlight of most cons—fans dress up in costumes, inspired either by particular works of science fiction or science fiction themes. The shows are elaborate and beautiful, and the costumers compete in different categories, such as best group presentation or best reenactment. Panel discussions provide a keystone to the con life. Writers, critics, artists, and fans make presentations and discuss topics related to science fiction. Such panels range from the serious, such as "Postmodernism and Science Fiction," to the humorous "Why Wesley Crusher Must Die" (character on *Star Trek: The Next Generation*). Cons have many book-signings where fans can discuss with writers what they like and dislike about their work. A con is a lively and fun introduction to the wild and crazy world of science fiction. Cons are usually advertised in science fiction magazines and local newspapers. The World Con is particularly important because the people who attend (or at least pay the membership fee) vote for the Hugo Awards. Named after Hugo Gernsback, an important and influential science fiction editor and publisher, the Hugo Award is given annually for best novel, short story, and so forth. Winning a Hugo is considered good for the winner's book sales. "Hugo-Award winner" is often printed across the covers of the winner's books. The genre's other major award, the Nebula, is awarded annually by the Science Fiction and Fantasy Writers of America, a smaller and more elite group (only published writers of fiction or criticism can join). While other popular genres, such as romance, have similar conventions and fanzines, the science fiction tradition involves more activity and a longer history.

CHARACTERISTICS OF SCIENCE FICTION

The unique world surrounding science fiction is reflected in its literature. Only science fiction uses extrapolation and cognitive estrangement. Extrapolation is a term taken from geometry, in which a set of points is used to draw a curve that goes beyond the points. The extended line is an extrapolation from the known points. Speculating from what exists to what might exist is an important quality of science fiction. Science fiction writers can take a scientific or sociological development and extrapolate it into the future. For example, McCaffrey's dragons are an extrapolation of genetic engineering, and space travel could be seen as an extrapolation of plane travel. Similarly, galactic empires could be seen as an extrapolation of the British Empire. H. G. Wells uses this technique in *The War of the Worlds*, in which Martians invade Earth in the same way that the British invaded other countries during the period of colonization. Extrapolation keeps science fiction located in issues and ethics that are a part of contemporary human culture.

Cognitive estrangement, or defamiliarization, is another key concept in science fiction. Literary theorist Darko Suvin bases this idea on the work of Viktor Shklovosky, a Russian theorist. Suvin has popularized Shklovoky's idea about making the familiar seem new and strange. While defamiliarization can occur in realistic fiction, this sense of estrangement appears at its most intense in science fiction. For example, Octavia Butler defamiliarizes not only the biological process, but also our attitudes toward reproduction and childbirth in the chilling Nebula-Award winning story about a pregnant male, "Bloodchild." Because a female alien impregnates the human male on her planet, we are estranged from our usual sentimental attitude toward mothering. Butler's "Bloodchild" allows the reader to see the familiar—childbirth—from a new angle. Similarly, McCaffrey defamiliarizes our sense of what makes us human by creating a character—Helva—who is both human and a space ship. The main character, a cyborg (part human and part machine), forces us to think about how we define humanity and femininity.

Science fiction also has developed the form known as the "shared universe," which can be either open or closed. A shared universe describes a setting and characters created by one another, but then written about by other writers. The proliferating Star Trek books provide one example of a shared universe; there is much professional and amateur writing about the characters of the television show. Shared universes have also been created as anthologies or book series, and a variety of writers create stories or books in a common setting. When characters and setting are copyrighted, the original author "owns" them. For example, Isaac Asimov created a new idea of robots and certain characters that have since been written about with his permission by other writers.

McCaffrey participates with other writers in a version of the shared universe. She and other writers, such as S. M. Sterling, expand her brain ship concept (see Chapter 5). McCaffrey takes more responsibility for her ideas than other writers who sometimes only allow their names to be used and do none of the writing in "shared universe" novels. In describing these works, she makes it clear that the final responsibility is always hers. "I would write the outline of the proposed novel and they [coauthors] would have the option to add any elements that came to them as they wrote, . . . but I did the final editing" (E-mail 4-12-95). Science fiction writers have a tradition of collaboration, where authors work together to create new characters and settings. McCaffrey and Elizabeth Ann Scarborough collaborate on *The Powers* series (see Chapter 10). No other genre involves as much collaboration and emphasis on the shared universe as science fiction.

Science fiction frequently involves robots, aliens, space travel, and the future. These features are more specific than the theoretical bases discussed previously, but they are no less important to the genre. Most people probably think of robots and space ships when they think of science fiction. Robots (machines that can function independently), androids (robots that look human), and cyborgs (creatures that are part human and part machine) all make science fiction exciting and bizarre. But they also serve another function: to help us decide what we mean by "human." Isaac Asimov's classic *I, Robot* is credited with changing our sense of robots as negative and threatening to a more positive view. Asimov created the Three Laws of Robotics, which state that robots must obey humans, must protect humans, and must protect themselves without violating the first two laws. Asimov's robots are the friends and protectors of humans. McCaffrey's brain ships and cities follow Asimov's beneficent version of robots, and like his creations they have to face prejudice. Robots, androids, and cyborgs provide a way to defamiliarize the plights of subordinate groups dealing with hostile and dangerous dominant groups.

Aliens also enable a discussion of trust and mistrust, prejudice and tolerance. While robots, androids, and cyborgs are usually created by humans, aliens are autonomous and perhaps even more threatening because of their difference from humans. The "first contact" story, in which humans and aliens first meet, is a classic device in science fiction. Through the first meeting, humans and aliens are tested: Can they be trusted? Will they behave ethically and responsibly? A classic example of "first contact" is the 1950s film, *The Day the Earth Stood Still*, based on the science fiction story "Farewell to the Master" by Harry Bates. In this film, a peaceful alien ambassador comes to Earth, but he is shot by a paranoid human. The movie shows how important first contact is, and how humans must overcome their prejudice and suspicion of difference in order to reap the benefits of contact with advanced aliens. McCaffrey uses first contact as the premise of her *Doona Series*, and includes first contact dilemmas in several other series.

Space travel is another standard ingredient in science fiction. With space travel, humans have a freedom unknown to us now, and some of our world's problems are solved by having other planets and galaxies to explore. For example, overpopulation and cultural differences can be reduced if humans can colonize other planets. In McCaffrey's *The Doona* series, the planet Doona allows "misfits" to develop a new society and at the same time to relieve congestion and pollution on Earth through the colonization of Doona. Science fiction's optimism can usually be found in stories that include space travel.

Equally optimistic and pessimistic are science fictions set in the future. Science fiction contains utopias (perfect worlds that don't exist) and dystopias (the worst of all possible worlds). Sometimes a science fiction novel like Marge Piercy's *Women on the Edge of Time* contains both. Piercy's time traveling heroine sees a vision of two alternate futures: In the utopia women and men "co-mother" children and live in equality, and humans live harmoniously with nature. In the dystopian future, the natural world is destroyed, and women are slaves. In Piercy's novel, and in other science fiction, writers suggest that whether we have a utopia or a dystopia in the future depends on the actions of the science fiction readers. Our actions today will result in the future being a utopia, dystopia, or a combination of these two. Utopias and dystopias allow science fiction writers to point to certain problems and extrapolate from them, as in the science fiction film, *Soylent Green*. In this dystopian film, overpopulation leads to humans becoming cannibals. Another example of a utopia would be Ursula K. Le Guin's *Always Coming Home*, in which a group of humans renounce male domination and find a way to live harmoniously with the land.

THE HISTORY OF SCIENCE FICTION

Modern science fiction begins with Mary Wollstonecraft Shelley's *Frankenstein* (1818). Shelley's work began the modern fascination with the scientist and (usually) his works. One of the most popular novels and ideas of the past two centuries, *Frankenstein* has the distinction of being the only single-authored text to become a myth. The word "Frankenstein" has become a part of the English language and is frequently used to describe the monster, or any creature created by science that is out of control of its creator. Subsequent science fiction was popular throughout the Victorian era in both England and the United States. For example, a belief in science and its ability to improve human existence marks such works as Edward Bellamy's *Looking Backward* (1888), a utopia set in the future that was so popular that there were even Looking Backward clubs. At the same time, pessimism about social change and industrialization defines such works as Edward Bulwer Lytton's *The Coming Race* (1871), which ends with the threat of a new species usurping humanity's rule of the Earth. At the end of the nineteenth century, H. G. Wells looked toward the immense changes that science would bring and used science fiction to criticize British colonialism in novels like *The Time Machine* (1895) and *The War of the Worlds* (1898).

The twentieth century has seen the flourishing of science fiction magazines. The production of cheap paper from wood pulp made magazines inexpensive—such journals were known as the pulps. Especially in the United States, such magazines flourished, in part because they pirated works by European and English authors. Both art and fiction were commissioned for the pulps at very cheap rates. Sometimes an artist would create a cover and then a writer would pen a story that fit the artwork. In the 1940s and 1950s, science fiction magazines helped create what many critics and writers call the "Golden Age" of science fiction. Writers like Isaac Asimov, Robert Heinlein, and Arthur C. Clarke began their careers writing for these magazines.

Many female science fiction writers, like C. L. Moore and Leigh Brackett, used male or genderless pseudonyms (false names). This practice continues with writers like James Tiptree, Jr., Andre Norton, and C. J. Cherryh. While there were few female humans in the pulp stories or art, female aliens appeared repeatedly in 1940s and 1950s science fiction. Such creatures helped keep alive an interest and fascination with gender in science fiction.

More recently, science fiction has experienced other trends, such as the New Wave movement of the 1960s, which stresses that science fiction should be taken seriously as literature, and includes elements of 1960s counterculture—drugs, sex, and the media. Cyberpunk, a school of science fiction writing that became popular in the 1980s, focuses on futures in which large global industrial and political units control society and rely on computer networks. In this future, humans are altered to interface with and become part of computer technology. Only one female writer, Pat Cadigan, is associated directly with this group of writers, but many others, including McCaffrey, now emphasize computer-human interface.

GENDER AND SCIENCE FICTION: THE FEMALE ALIEN

Science fiction is usually considered a masculine genre, written by men for a male audience. As its name suggests, science fiction has been associated with science, and science has been and still remains an arena dominated by men. However, science itself, its practice, and the technologies it produces are not exclusively male. Because science is frequently used to justify social customs and practices and government policies, it is very important that the group of writers who most influence our attitudes toward science reflect the full range of human beings. While the field of science still does not contain representative proportions of women, science fiction begins to do so. Unfortunately, science fiction still has to live up to its potential to include other groups, but there are important African-American science fiction writers like Octavia Butler and Samuel Delany. While science fiction cannot predict the future, it can and does shape our thinking about what scientists should do. Certain ideas such as space travel were once only fiction; perhaps ideas like equality between the sexes and races will someday also be reality.

As in other fields, gender shapes and defines our understanding of science and science fiction. Science and science fiction are still divided into "hard" and "soft" categories that reflect a masculine perspective that "hard" is better. The hard sciences—natural sciences such as biology—are supposedly more objective and rigorous, while the so-called "soft" social sciences such as anthropology are considered more subjective. Science fiction explores the social sciences, and expands them to include psionics, which can be defined as mental sciences—telepathy (mind reading), telekinesis (the ability to move objects using only the powers of the mind), teleportation (the ability to move your body through space without using your muscles), and so on. McCaffrey helps confound the artificial and sexist distinctions between "hard" and "soft" science and science fiction by clearly identifying psionics as scientifically verified and amplified in her fictions. Careful readers of her novels realize, for example, that the dragons she creates are genetically altered creatures. Even their telepathic qualities were carefully bred into them.

What may seem magical in science fiction may just be science that is beyond our contemporary reach or understanding. One of science fiction's most respected writers, Arthur C. Clarke, writes that "any insufficiently advanced technology is indistinguishable from magic" (Pournelle 245). John Campbell, a distinguished and influential editor who worked with McCaffrey, also believed "Science, is the magic that works" (Campbell 5). This attitude toward science and magic allows science fiction writers to reclaim magic *as* science. Especially important for women, valorizing or validating magic has a historical dimension. Similar in nature, magic and science have been criticized or praised according to the sex of the practitioner. So-called "witches" in Europe were persecuted from the fourteenth to the seventeenth century, in part because they posed a threat to the emerging field of medicine. Witches competed with doctors and priests for the custom of the people. Witches actually practiced what we today call the scientific method—trial and experiment—and witches used many drugs we now use, such as belladonna, ergot, and digitalis (Ehrenreich and English). Both male writers like Frank Herbert and female writers like Anne McCaffrey use "witches" in their fiction. In so doing, these science fiction writers ask us to reconsider the past—historical witches—and the future—what the universe might be like if we knew how to control magical powers.

In general, however, women writers tend to depict witches and magic more positively than do male writers. For example, Frank Herbert's witches, the Bene Gesserit, actually pose a threat to the male hero in *Dune*. In contrast, Andre Norton (pseudonym for Mary Alice Norton), creates a world, in *Witch World*, where witches rescue a male hero. McCaffrey cites Andre Norton as one of her favorite writers and credits Norton with coming up with the title for one of McCaffrey's *Pern* books, *The White Dragon*. McCaffrey's female heroines have mysterious witchlike powers and are frequently described as "witches."

A witch is a type of female alien in a literary tradition that begins with Mary Wollstonecraft Shelley's *Frankenstein*. In Shelley's novel, there are no central female characters, and the female mate for Frankenstein's "monster" never even draws a breath. Victor Frankenstein is so horrified by the prospect of the monster reproducing, and of the possibility that the female creature would prefer him to the monster, that he destroys her body in disgust. This female creature is the first of a long series of female aliens, creatures who are frightening not only because of their superhuman powers, but also because of their ability to reproduce. The creature in *Aliens*, the tremendously popular science fiction film, provides one contemporary example of a depiction of a female alien. While in early, classic science fiction by Shelley, Edward Bulwer Lytton, H. G.

Wells and others, the female alien is depicted as a threat and a danger to male heroes, from the nineteenth century on, women writers, such as Charlotte Perluns Gilman and Mary E. Bradley Lane, have depicted powerful and likeable female aliens. Traditionally feminine traits such as mothering, nurturing, reproductive powers, and sexual attractiveness to human males characterize the female alien. In many cases, the female alien is not even humanoid, but she still represents human females because of her feminine qualities. The brain ship, Helva, from McCaffrey's *The Ship Who Sang*, provides one example of a female alien. Her body has been encapsulated in a ship, but despite her lack of a fully functioning human body Helva is still decidedly feminine.

As Helva and other female aliens demonstrate, the patterns of science fiction provide a starting point for an entirely different view of the future. By focusing on the special position of women as reproducers of the human race and of human culture, women writers can imagine a world based on feminine values of nurturing, interdependence, and community. Through the patterns of science fiction, women writers create worlds and even universes of their own. They ask us to imagine a utopian future in which women can control their own bodies, and in which men and women are equal. Through the traditional settings of science fiction, writers present feminist alternatives to patriarchal societies and male-dominated science. Ursula K. Le Guin has said that "science fiction is the mythology of the modern world"; it is a mythology now transformed by women writers like McCaffrey.

Dragonflight

Dragonflight may justly be considered Anne McCaffrey's most important work, for with this novel she began *The Dragonriders of Pern*, her most famous series (see Chapter 4 for a discussion of the series). *Dragonflight* is important for a number of reasons. One of McCaffrey's notable achievements is that she won *both* the Hugo and Nebula Awards (see Chapter 2). The first woman writer to receive either award, McCaffrey did so with short fiction, "Weyr Search" (Hugo) and "Dragon Rider" (Nebula), which was later expanded into the novel *Dragonflight*. Second, this novel has received a great deal of critical attention. Third, in *Dragonflight* McCaffrey most completely develops the plot that will serve as a model for the other books in the series. Fourth, and perhaps most important, *Dragonflight* contains character, plot, and themes that are representative of McCaffrey's work in general. And finally, the book deserves its own chapter because it is a rich and complex text.

McCaffrey's *The Dragonriders of Pern* does for dragons what Isaac Asimov's Robot series does for robots—it establishes dragons as sentient, competent, and caring companions and creatures with a believable scientific explanation for their existence. Every aspect of the other novels in the series can be traced back to *Dragonflight*, for in this first novel in the series, McCaffrey has a clear and consistent outline of what dragons do and what they are. McCaffrey's dragons are those by which all other dragons are measured; she has taken them from fantasy and made them an important part of science fiction.

PLOT DEVELOPMENT

Dragonflight begins as many of McCaffrey's novels do, *in medias res* (in the middle of a story). This structure was common to epic poetry, such as John Milton's *Paradise Lost*, so McCaffrey draws on a time-honored tradition for her plot and immediately captures her reader's interest. McCaffrey begins in the middle in two ways: the novel describes events in the middle of the planet Pern's history, and events in the middle of the heroine's life.

Many science fiction novels begin with the colonization of a planet, but *Dragonflight* depicts the events that occur long after the initial exploration and development of Pern. The third planet orbiting the star Rukbat in the constellation of Sagittarius, Pern is special because of its suitability for human habitation. The Earth is the third planet from our sun, and, as far as we know, the only planet in our system suitable for human habitation. This parallel to the Earth strengthens the reader's identification with Pern's human inhabitants. Pern has the same unique potential for sentient life that our planet does, and the same problems (human greed, politics). McCaffrey makes the setting exotic, yet familiar because it is in a part of space named for the Zodiac sign of Sagittarius. When the novel opens, Pern has been colonized so long ago that its human inhabitants do not even remember their Earth history, and their technology has devolved to a craft and farm society. In a thought-provoking introduction, McCaffrey situates Pern as a society that has myths and legends like the Earth.

The book begins with these words, "When is a legend legend? Why is a myth a myth?" (xi). The rest of the novel answers these questions, and the introduction explains how Pern's origins and history produce myth and legend. The Earthly origin of the planet's first settlers has now been forgotten by their descendents, but the reader is informed of the Pern connection to Earth. While their Earthly origins are no longer even legends, there are legends and myths centered on the dragons and their riders. As the plot of *Dragonflight* reveals, remembering and using these legends and myths will save the planet and its inhabitants from destruction.

This introduction situates the novel as science fiction and lets readers know more about the development of Pern than its inhabitants do. In this privileged position, we want to know even more about Pern's development. How did the colonists get to this state? How did they evolve dragons? Why did they choose Pern? Some answers and clues are provided in *Dragonflight*, but the full history of Pern fills more than a dozen books, with more to follow (see Chapter 4). Two books of Pern history have been coauthored by McCaffrey: *The Dragonlover's Guide to Pern* with Jody Lynn Nye, and *The People of Pern* with Robin Wood. While these two books make for enjoyable secondary reading, it is the pleasure of discovering more about Pern and dragons that draws readers to the novels.

In *Dragonflight*, the reader makes discoveries along with the young heroine, Lessa. The only surviving member of a ruling family, Lessa hides in a community called a Weyr that used to house dragons and their riders. She uses her mental powers and trickery to sabotage the usurper who killed her family and who now exploits her family's land. Lessa is descended from dragonriders, but she knows nothing about them. Her ignorance stems from her position as an outcast, but also because dragons have become less important to Pernese society in general. The number of dragons has dwindled so that there is only one active Weyr (home for dragons and their riders) and only one queen dragon. Lessa's ignorance makes her the ideal stand-in for the reader; like Lessa, we are attracted to the dragons, but know nothing about them. As Lessa makes her discoveries and bonds with a dragon, the reader vicariously experiences the pleasures of flying and communing with a dragon.

Readers find out, as Lessa and her lover F'lar do, that dragons have a very important function in Pern society. Periodically, Pern is invaded by a mycorrhizoid spore or a fungus made of threadlike tubes known as Thread. Lethal to plant and animal life, Thread burrows into both ground and flesh; it can destroy the planet. Pernese use fire-breathing dragons to destroy Thread before it strikes the planet. Because Thread has not fallen for hundreds of years, however, most of Pern has become complacent and the dragonriders have lost their preeminence and some of their knowledge about how to combat Thread. As F'lar, a dragonrider, identifies Lessa as a candidate for a queen dragonrider, Thread is about to threaten the planet again. Only the rediscovery and repopulation of the world with dragons will save Pern.

The reader is invited to unravel the mystery of the dragons and the solution to Pern's plight with the help of clues from ballads that precede each chapter. These brief and tantalizing verses describe dragons and their role in combatting Thread. Like the characters, readers find the solution through these clues, which teach dragons and their riders to travel not only through space, but also through time to recruit dragon-riders from the past to save Pern's future. McCaffrey thus answers the questions posed in the preface about the importance of legend and fairy tales—it is the ballads that provide the way to rescue Pern from extinction. The excerpts she uses in the novel's structure are not only entertaining, but also central to the plot.

Using questions and supplying Pern's history in the introduction draw the reader into the world of Pern. The introduction works as preparation, as a hook, and then the ballads provide the answers. This structure smoothly integrates the reader into Pern. Just as we are introduced to the exciting and unique features of the dragons and their riders, however, we discover that Pern is threatened with extinction by the burrowing Thread. As its name suggests, the Thread ties together the plot and the characters. Their differences temporarily put aside in the face of danger, the Pernese work together to fight their common enemy. The reappearance of the Thread immediately raises the stature of the dragons and dragonriders—once again, they are needed to save the planet. Just as the dragons and dragonriders discover a sense of power, the reader discovers his or her power by discovering the centrality of the ballads to the plot.

With the exciting plot of an embattled planet, McCaffrey has pulled millions of readers into the thrilling world of Pern. Through the pattern of discovery, challenge, and resolution, she moves the plot along quickly. Lessa is central to this process. As the book opens, Lessa has just awakened from sleep, an activity that prepares her for other awakenings: to dragons, to her sexuality, and to her special role in the redemption of Pern. We meet Lessa as we do Pern, in the middle of her history. Lessa has already endured the capture of her land and the murder of her entire family, and she has survived another decade, or 10 Turns as Pern years are called. A young woman, she has yet to find her true calling or friends. She is aware of her mental powers to manipulate other people, but she is not yet aware of her ability to communicate with all dragons, a quality no other human has. Like Pern itself, we meet Lessa at a critical turning point.

CHARACTER DEVELOPMENT

As the first character we meet, and as a character with the critical skill needed to save Pern, Lessa can be described as the novel's protagonist. She undergoes many changes in the course of the novel, and much of the novel is told from her point of view. In the beginning, Lessa is friendless and alone, with only the affection of a watch-wher, a degraded version of a dragon/watch dog. A greedy lord had attacked her family's Hold years ago while everyone was sleeping, and her entire family was killed. In the wake of this tragedy, Lessa grows to womanhood alone. She labors as a drudge and avoids attention, for two reasons. First, the Lord Fax, who has taken over her land, would kill her if he knew she was alive. Fax had her family killed so that he could take over their Hold. Second, Lessa needs obscurity in order to continue her act of sabotage. She lives only for revenge and has not thought beyond Fax's death, which she hopes to arrange. Using her psionic, or mental, powers, Lessa blurs her features and remains dirty and unkempt in order to survive unnoticed. She also subtly influences people to behave as she wishes. For example, when F'lar and Fax arrive at Ruatha Hold (Lessa's family Hold) together, Lessa exacerbates their rivalry and incites them to a duel. Whether F'lar or Fax wins, Lessa figures she will be the winner. If Fax kills the dragonrider, he will be in trouble, and if, as she suspects, the dragonrider kills Fax, she will be able to claim her Hold for herself. After the dragonrider F'lar fights and kills Fax, Lessa does not know how to treat him or any other humans. She has, after all, lived a precarious and solitary existence from age 10 to 21. She has not been well socialized.

After F'lar persuades Lessa to leave Ruatha Hold for Benden Weyr, the dragonrider's home, Lessa realizes she has value in the eyes of other people. She cleans herself up and discovers that she is attractive. She begins to see herself as a part of Benden Weyr. F'lar has been drawn to Lessa by her spirit, and he believes that she will be a good candidate to ''Impress'' the queen egg, an egg that contains a queen dragon, treasured for her ability to reproduce. The term *Impress* carries three connotations: first, that of a young animal bonding with a human. Second, humans must Impress or be seen as worthy by a dragon. Third, any human who Impresses a dragon becomes a dragonrider and rises in status. Dragonriders Impress dragons at birth, imprinting and bonding with them; it is the dragon who chooses which human to be Impressed by. Dragon and rider communicate telepathically, and the dragonrider cares for and feeds his or her dragon. To be chosen by a dragon is a rare honor; to be on the field with just-born dragons about to be Impressed can be dangerous, for they are so large and heedless of any human but the one they choose.

Lessa survives the Impression, and the baby queen dragon, Ramoth, chooses her. Ramoth provides Lessa with unconditional love; their telepathic bond gives Lessa the reassurance and support that she needs. In addition, flying the queen provides Lessa with status as one of the leaders of Benden Weyr. Lessa and Ramoth's relationship is a development of the relationship that Lessa has had with the watch-wher. But while the watch-wher was more like a pet, Ramoth is Lessa's equal. This egalitarian relationship functions as a model for Lessa's relationship with humans.

At first, Lessa's relationships with other humans do not go smoothly. Lessa discovers too late that she admires Lady Gemma, Fax's reluctant wife. First she is so angry with Fax that she crushes Gemma's hands as Gemma endures childbirth. Gemma dies before Lessa realizes that her hatred of Gemma was unfair. After she becomes a dragonrider, Lessa continually plagues R'gul, the Weyrleader who instructs her in dragon lore and ballads. By questioning current practices and the meaning of the teaching songs, Lessa aggravates the dragon leader. She doesn't trust R'gul, especially after F'lar replaces him as Weyrleader. Lessa is jealous of Kylara, another dragonrider candidate, and F'lar suspects that Lessa uses her mental powers to keep Kylara in awe of her. Lessa and F'lar have a stormy relationship; he does not treat her as an equal and tries to keep her from flying Ramoth "*between*."

"*Between*" is a kind of no space that dragons can navigate through, but it is also dangerous because staying *between* for too long means death for both dragon and rider. Flying *between* signifies maturity for both dragon and rider, so F'lar's postponement of Lessa and Ramoth's flying *between* keeps the pair bound to the weyr. F'lar also does not think that queens should fly against Thread. Ostensibly he wants to protect Ramoth, the only surviving queen dragon, but this prohibition keeps Ramoth and Lessa dependent and helpless. F'lar patronizes Lessa, but as Lessa changes and matures, so does F'lar. Both must learn to trust and to take risks. Lessa and F'lar end up as lovers when their dragons mate. Because of their close telepathic links, dragonriders feel drawn to a sexual relationship with each other when their dragons mate. It is almost as if they have no choice. However, Lessa and F'lar eventually develop their sexual relationship independent of their dragons. To do so, however, they must learn to trust and respect each other.

In an insightful analysis of Lessa and F'lar's relationship, Jane Donawerth discusses McCaffrey's use of the heterosexual romance plot. Donawerth points out that McCaffrey uses a double narration to give us both characters' perspective in unusual ways. For example, she explains that "after Lessa and philosophy's first sexual union [we see] from F'lar's point of view, but not so that we may sympathize with him: he is at this point, briefly, the 'dumb' male narrator, parodied" (45). Donawerth discusses other science fiction writers who use a "dumb" male narrator, and multiple narrators, but stresses that this pattern became common after the 1960s, when McCaffrey uses it. Even though the narration may be told from the male character's point of view, McCaffrey still directs the reader to sympathize with Lessa. Lessa, then, remains the heroine even as McCaffrey suggests the importance of men and women working together. Donawerth argues that the need to protect the planet from Thread requires "adaptability and collaboration" (16), qualities that Lessa and F'lar develop in the course of their romance. The parallel between plot and Lessa and F'lar's character development stresses the same theme.

Lessa and F'lar demonstrate other important character traits. F'lar recognizes that Lessa is stronger than other women because she has survived harsh circumstances. "Adversity, uncertainty; those were the conditions that bred the qualities that F'lar wanted" (*Dragonflight* 7). Lessa's intelligence and independence are also confirmed by F'lar's dragon, Mnementh (132). The dragon seems "besotted" with Lessa, from F'lar's perspective, and Mnementh wants to include Lessa in adventures long before F'lar fully realizes Lessa's skills. To be appreciated by a dragon is the highest compliment, for they are extraordinarily perceptive judges of character. Lessa's sensitivity to danger, her sense of humor, and her willingness to take risks all vindicate F'lar's choice of her as a candidate for Impressing a queen dragon. Lessa's premonitions about impending danger support F'lar's insistence that Thread will again fall on Pern. Humor might seem less important than the other qualities, but Lessa uses her sense of humor to make important points. For example, she makes a pun about being "hidebound" when the actual clues to how previous generations fought Thread are on parchment made from hides (176). As Lessa, F'lar, Mnementh, and Ramoth contemplate flying back in time, the dragons and Lessa joke, relieving tension before deciding on an important mission (254). Finally, Lessa's courage and intrepidness suit her as the first dragonrider to travel through time. She is brave enough to fly Ramoth where no dragon has gone before.

F'lar himself has many of the same qualities as Lessa, as well as a desire to lead and the intelligence to decipher clues about how to fight Thread (206). F'lar also exemplifies the qualities of a scientist. He is indefatigable in his research and he studies old records until he figures out when Thread will fall. A good fighter and tactician, F'lar is already a leader of 12 dragonriders. A perceptive judge of character, F'lar realizes Lessa's potential even under all the grime. F'lar demonstrates great sensitivity to a dragonrider who has lost his dragon, and even has trouble speaking after meeting the bereft dragonrider. It takes Lessa, however, to tame F'lar's arrogance. Over the course of the novel, he learns to temper his self-assurance and to work with her.

Both F'lar and Lessa exemplify the moral at the end: "Living was struggling to do the impossible—to succeed, or die, knowing you had tried" (208). This noble precept evokes the notion of a Romantic quest, an epic struggle. Here again McCaffrey's themes reflect the structure of the novel. Like an epic poem, the novel begins *in medias res* and its themes are of epic quality. McCaffrey focuses on the quest of special individuals, Lessa and F'lar, to protect their world, and also to acquire new and possibly dangerous knowledge.

THEMES

In *Dragonflight*, McCaffrey uses plot and character to emphasize a number of themes. Fax's unattractiveness and quick demise show the dangers of greed and its consequences. The unique dragon/human bond reveals the importance of mutual respect, trust, and caring. Through Lessa and to a lesser degree, F'lar, McCaffrey valorizes the figure of the outsider. She shows that the outsider can have something valuable to offer his or her society, and such people should not be treated unfairly. Through the history of Pern's fight against Thread, McCaffrey stresses the importance of change and flexibility; without openness to innovation, the dragonriders would not have been able to save Pern from destruction. Finally, and perhaps most important from a literary perspective, McCaffrey reveals the importance of art in promoting change and flexibility. Art literally provides the clues that save the planet from Thread. As a science fiction writer, McCaffrey knows the importance of science (the engineered dragons), but she also believes that art and science should work together.

Greed

Dragonflight reveals the dangers of being greedy. Fax, the tyrant who kills Lessa's family, has been motivated by greed. He takes over not only her land, but also that of a number of other holdings. Fax has more land than he can properly manage, and his greed is rewarded with his early death. Cruel to his wife and covetous of others' goods (7), Fax lets greed dominate his decisions. Two of Fax's underlings who run Ruatha Hold are also greedy, and Lessa uses their greed to lead them to premature deaths (30). Other lords repeat Fax's mistake, though in less brutal ways. Wanting to keep more of their goods, the lords at first stint the portion due the dragonriders, and then threaten to end their tithing to the dragonriders, who do not have the time to farm or practice a craft other than dragonriding. This greed threatens all of Pern, for without the dragons and dragonriders, the lords' forests and fields would go unprotected. The dragonriders are warned not to be greedy by one of the teaching ballads. "Dragonman, avoid excess;/Greed will bring the Weyr distress" (22). The novel's plot emphasizes the importance of sharing your wealth and goods for the benefit of all. Greed creates an unequal and unbalanced society that becomes problematic for all classes. In addition, greed threatens all of Pern because short-sighted greed prompts the lords to try to rebel against the dragonrider's maintenance.

Animal-Human Cooperation

The novel stresses the importance of cooperating with and respecting other species. The dragon/human relationship is a model, full of mutual respect, trust, and love. Through loving their dragons and taking care of them, Lessa and F'lar find a model for their own relationship. They give and receive much from their dragons. The dragonriders supply food, oil the dragons' itchy hides, and give their companionship. In addition to providing affection and understanding, the dragons enable their riders to fly. In a world without airplanes, the dragons provide their riders with freedom, mobility, and status. Most importantly, the dragons protect the planet and all its inhabitants from complete destruction. By training and caring for dragons, humans reap partners who work untiringly to protect human homes, lives, and crops. By giving Lessa's watch-wher such a prominent position in the novel, McCaffrey implies that her readers should respect and admire all animals. The humble watch-wher has less intelligence than a human, but nonetheless, it behaves nobly when it gives its life to protect Lessa. The dragons recognize this when they mourn the watch-wher's death by wailing. McCaffrey implies that humans should respect and care for animals because of the possibility of mutual benefits.

The Outsider

Throughout *Dragonflight*, McCaffrey emphasizes the importance of the outsider. Lessa is an outsider in several ways. First, she is alone, without a family. Only her bond with the watch-wher enables her to hide in its dark and filthy lair as Fax slaughters the rest of her family. Her job in her former home is that of a drudge, a lowly servant, whom no one pays any attention to. While she has some dragonrider blood, she is not from Benden Weyr, the only surviving hold of dragons. Historically, dragonriders had been welcome at all Holds, and through affairs had mingled their genes with those of the Holders. While she may be related biologically, Lessa knows no one in Benden Weyr, and its routines and society are unfamiliar to her. But it is Lessa who saves Pern by learning how to travel through time and by finding reinforcements for the group of dragonriders.

F'lar too is an outsider. At the beginning of the book, he is not yet the dragonleader or weyrleader, and he has odd ideas about where to search for promising candidates to Impress dragons. As a dragonrider in a Pern society that devalues dragonriders, he is not welcome in many Holds, and the Lord Fax even tries to kill him. The dragonriders as a group are outside the rest of Pern society, and there is even an attempt at rebellion by the ungrateful lords of Holds against the dragonriders. The lords become greedy after hundreds of years without Thread, and they decide to stop providing goods for the dragonhold. Quelled by the dragonriders' quick action, the rebellion and its leaders look foolish when they must turn to the dragonriders to save them from Thread. But it is the dragonriders who redeem themselves by saving their entire world. McCaffrey warns of the dangers of dismissing even a lowly drudge, because she may turn out to be like Lessa and have wonderful and important gifts to offer her society.

The outsider's perspective may prove beneficial, too. Because Lessa is not from Benden Weyr, she can look at dragonriding from a fresh perspective. Her openness enables her to discover how to time travel. Time travel is critical to the survival of Pern, as it enables Lessa to bring other dragonriders forward in time to fight Thread.

Change and Flexibility

Lessa and F'lar's flexibility and willingness to change reveals the value of these qualities. Without their adaptability, Pern itself would have perished. Lessa creatively decides that she can travel through time, and her willingness to try something new is rewarded. To a lesser degree, she demonstrates this same quality when she is able to abandon her plan of revenge and leaves her land for another chance—the chance to Impress a queen dragon. Her risk-taking then is rewarded with the love and affection of Ramoth, a queen dragon. Similarly, F'lar realizes he must fight Thread in new ways. Instead of repeating old, now inadequate fighting techniques, F'lar searches out old records for clues of new ways to fight Thread. F'lar also is the only dragonrider to try to search in unusual places for Impression candidates. His adventuresomeness is rewarded with Lessa, who not only Impresses the queen dragon but also becomes his partner and ally. Lessa's flexibility saves her life when her Hold is attacked. Flexibility and willingness to grow also allow Lessa and F'lar to establish a fulfilling relationship.

The Importance of Literature and Art

Significantly, one source of creativity and salvation for Pern turns out to be various forms of art. Both Lessa and F'lar find clues in the Teaching Ballads, songs that each dragonrider is supposed to learn by rote. Most seem to think that these songs are mere entertainments, but Lessa especially realizes their deeper meaning. The sprinkling of brief excerpts from ballads throughout the text reinforces the reader's sense of their importance. The ballads prefigure the chapter's events, and they also set a mood and tone for the novel. Robinton, the Master Harper, also proves to be one of Lessa and F'lar's most valuable allies, so not only the songs, but also the singers provide assistance to the dragonriders' quest.

Here McCaffrey draws on her own experiences as a singer, even to modeling Robinton after one of her instructors. (see Chapter 1).

McCaffrey emphasizes some of the ballads more than others. For example, the lines "Honor those the dragons heed/ In thought and favor, word and deed./ Worlds are lost and worlds are saved/ From the dangers dragon-braved" appear repeatedly, validating F'lar's claim of the importance of dragons in combating Thread. The ballads also contain advice to Holders to keep their stone settlements free from foliage that could feed Thread and other specific clues about how to fight Thread. Using *between* to escape Thread and watching the Red Star to determine when Thread will fall appear in the teaching songs. The ballads can even make the deadly Thread seem beautiful: "A strand of silver/ In the sky" (175). Throughout the novel, McCaffrey reveals the transformative and informative power of art. It is one such song, the Question Song, that provides the key to Pern's salvation (234). The song explains that a group of dragonriders had gone ahead. Lessa correctly analyzes the song as referring to time travel, which then sends her to another piece of art, the tapestry in her family's Hold.

Perhaps the most important piece of art in the novel is the tapestry that Lessa interprets. It provides a model for a flamethrower that can be recreated to sear Thread. More importantly, Lessa sees not just one detail of a tool, but the whole picture. An impressive and beautiful piece, the work is described by a character as "A masterweaver's work. . . . It took a man's life to set up the loom, a craft's whole effort to complete" (255). It has lasted, bright and vivid, for hundreds of years. The tapestry provides her with the idea to travel back in time, as well as the specific coordinates she needs to guide Ramoth in their journey to the past. Art contains valuable information that only requires a skilled reader to discover. In addition to information, art also inspires and sustains individuals and societies. The humble nature of these arts—popular ballads and needlework—suggests that McCaffrey means to valorize not only high art, but also popular forms of art like science fiction itself. Just as the art within the book produces important information, so does science fiction, through its themes and ideas.

ALTERNATE READING: FEMINIST CRITICISM

Feminism is a social movement for the social, political, and economic equality of women and men; one aspect of feminist literary criticism attempts to reach equality by focusing on female writers and characters.

Feminist literary criticism is a rich and diverse field with a long history. However, this literary movement emerged with particular strength in the late 1960s and early 1970s, just as McCaffrey was becoming a best-selling author. Feminist critics stress that gender, one's social identity as either male or female, is one of the most important defining qualities of a human life. It is, after all, the first question that is asked when a baby is born, and whether people are male or female affects every aspect of their existence. The issues of feminist literary criticism and feminism in general appear in McCaffrey's novels. Some feminist literary critics focus on women writers, or on female characters, or on language. McCaffrey's *Dragonflight* allows the exploration of all three topics.

As a female writer, McCaffrey invites a feminist analysis. Feminist critics would want to know how McCaffrey's experiences as a woman affect her writing. McCaffrey describes her mother as a brave and versatile woman, and asks, "Is it any wonder I write about strong women?" ("Retrospection" 22). Not surprisingly, all of McCaffrey's heroines are also extraordinary. Even though some of her heroines, like Lessa, live in worlds that are even more limiting for women than our own Earth, these female characters inevitably triumph over their sexist society. McCaffrey's female characters face adversity, as McCaffrey herself did. Her husband was not supportive of her writing and she has described herself as being "psychologically battered" (E-mail 3-9-95). Nevertheless, McCaffrey persisted in her writing and triumphed over her husband's criticism. Similarly, McCaffrey succeeded in the primarily male-dominated world of science fiction; she was the first woman to win the Hugo Award and the Nebula. McCaffrey's achievements make her a role model for other women writers and for her readers.

While some feminist critics look to the gender of the writer and make that the focus of their analysis, other feminist critics look to female characters. Again McCaffrey's work provides paradigmatic instances. Most of McCaffrey's protagonists are, like Lessa, female. In this regard alone, McCaffrey is part of a feminist movement within science fiction. The shift to female protagonists and to issues of concern to women, such as relationships rather than science alone, became widespread in the 1970s, so McCaffrey here too is a leader of change. In this regard, science fiction, like other genres, reflects the society in which it was produced. The effect of the women's movement can be seen in McCaffrey's novels. At the same time, McCaffrey should be credited with helping to make changes in our society by creating powerful heroines with whom female readers can identify. McCaffrey's heroines do not start out powerful, but end up so by the end of the novels. Through hard work, luck, and talent, Lessa escapes when her family is massacred, takes her revenge on their murderer, and finds a new and satisfying life for herself. Lessa also breaks new ground for all women when she insists on flying her queen, Ramoth, to fight Thread. While women had flown queens in battle before, the practice had lapsed. It took Lessa's courage and determination to make it possible for women to fly and fight again (reflecting the issue now as to whether women should fly combat missions in the military). While readers may not typically think of science fiction as a genre with realistic elements, Lessa serves as a believable and realistic role model. McCaffrey emphasizes that her heroines are intended to be believable characters rather than fairy tale characters: "My heroines are victims who show that they can survive whatever has victimized them. This is an important difference [from the Cinderella story] in both viewpoint and conclusion" (E-mail 3-9-95). McCaffrey's revision of the Cinderella plot is feminist in that it empowers the Cinderella figure.

While Lessa functions as a role model, she also works to shift the emphasis in science fiction away from male characters and traditionally masculine concerns (see Chapter 2). When male and female readers get caught up in *Dragonflight*, they identify with a feminine viewpoint. This shift in perspective enables the male reader to temporarily leave his gender behind. Only through fiction can humans experiment so widely with point of view, for we can also see the world from Ramoth's perspective. The queen dragon's physical needs and clear, direct understanding and love for Lessa make her an admirable and engaging character.

Part of this change in perspective is an emphasis on language. The telepathic communication between dragon and rider can be seen as feminine language. Some feminist critics see language itself as masculinized. They argue that our very ideas and thoughts are structured by the male-dominated words we use. McCaffrey offers telepathy as an alternative to traditional language. This mental power has traditionally been associated with women—witches—and has been considered magic. In *Dragonflight*, telepathic communication provides an instantaneous level of trust and love between dragon and rider. There can be no pretense or lies when they hear each other's thoughts. While telepathy is traditionally considered magical and hence associated with the feminine, McCaffrey emphasizes the gendering of telepathy through Lessa. Like Moreta, a famous dragonrider from the past, Lessa can hear *all* dragons, not just the dragon she Impressed. The only other character to have this talent is a young girl in *The Girl Who Heard Dragons*. That it is female characters who have this power in the greatest degree stresses its femininity. *Dragonflight* offers a subtle analysis of the gendering of language.

4

The Dragonriders of Pern Series

Anne McCaffrey's series *The Dragonriders of Pern* now numbers 13 books. If she satisfies her fans, McCaffrey will continue to write more about Pern, a planet colonized by humans and populated with lovable and engaging dragons. What makes *Dragonriders* so unique and compelling is McCaffrey's clever and original depiction of dragons not as mythical beasts, but as creatures bred and handled by humans. The scientific basis for the dragons makes the series believable and compelling as science fiction. We have always wanted a reason to believe in and love dragons; McCaffrey's science fiction makes such an engagement possible and plausible.

The Dragonriders of Pern is McCaffrey's longest and perhaps most famous series. It is for the short stories in this series that she won both the Hugo and the Nebula Awards (see Chapter 2). The series has also inspired many spin-offs, from plays to fanzines and merchandise. While McCaffrey has been pleased with the authorized developments of her creations, she is concerned that "there have been far too many infringements and violations" (E-mail 4-22-95) of her copyright. She requests that readers do not abuse copyright by using characters or settings from her books in unauthorized games or stories. McCaffrey is very specific about the details of Pern, especially the dragons. "Dragons come only in gold, bronze, brown, blue and green as dragon blood is copper-based" (E-mail 4-22-95). Even in such a detail as color, McCaffrey reveals her careful use of known science. While all of McCaffrey's books are extremely successful, *The Dragonriders of Pern* have out-sold her other novels (E-mail 4-22-95).

Dragonflight, *Dragonsinger*, and *Dragonsong* have all been produced on the stage (Hargreaves, *Anne Inez McCaffrey: Forty Years* 299–305). An atlas and gaming books based on *The Dragonriders of Pern* have been published, and there are also calendars, posters, a map, and even a number of songbooks of Pern. McCaffrey has also worked closely with two publications that explain and develop *The Dragonriders of Pern*: Jody Lynn Nye's *The Dragonlover's Guide to Pern* and Robin Wood's *The People of Pern*.

SERIES DEVELOPMENT

Throughout *The Dragonriders of Pern*, McCaffrey employs a variety of perspectives. In most of the novels, she uses an omniscient narrator, but in a few cases she uses a first-person narrative (*Nerilka's Story*). In some novels, she engages an adult perspective, including some explicit references to sexuality (*Moreta: Dragonlady of Pern*); in others, she draws on a series of young adult characters who encounter challenges and mature over the course of the novel (*The Harper Hall Trilogy: Dragonsong, Dragonsinger, Dragondrums*). The last five books (*Dragonsdawn, The Renegades of Pern, The Chronicles of Pern: First Fall, All the Weyrs of Pern, The Dolphins of Pern*) use a narrator who shifts, thus reflecting a number of the characters' thoughts, including the thoughts of dolphins. The combined effect of all 13 texts produces a fully-developed sense of a culture. In the list of novels on the flyleaf of the more recent books, McCaffrey clearly indicates her preference that readers encounter the novels in their order of publication. McCaffrey does not insist that they be read in chronological order, but in the order in which the novels were written. *Moreta* and *Nerilka's Story* are both preequals, set almost 1,500 years before the events of the first novel, *Dragonflight*. Her request to the reader is phrased so: "*The author respectfully suggests that books in the Pern series be read in the order that they were published. Which is: [book titles]*" (frontpiece, *The Renegades of Pern*). But the order that she signals makes sense, because McCaffrey builds upon the concepts and points of view presented in each novel. In order, the novels are: *Dragonflight*; *Dragonquest*; *The White Dragon*; *The Harper Hall Trilogy: Dragonsong, Dragonsinger, Dragondrums*; *Moreta: Dragonlady of Pern*; *Nerilka's Story*; *Dragonsdawn*; *The Renegades of*

Pern; The Chronicles of Pern: First Fall ("Rescue Run," the last story in *Chronicles* has also been published separately as a short book); *All the Weyrs of Pern*, and *The Dolphins of Pern*. (*The Girl Who Heard Dragons*, a collection of stories, contains only one story set in Pern). By *The Dolphins of Pern*, the most recent novel (1994), we have seen Pern from the perspective of members of all its major social groups: the Holds, the communities organized around a lord and his family, primarily engaged in agriculture; the Weyrs, the dragonrider communities that protect the Holds and in turn receive goods and food from the Holds; the Crafts, who preserve the knowledge and practice of skills, including music used for teaching and history. *The Renegades of Pern* focuses on a young trader outside any of its major institutions, completing our view of the culture. *The Chronicles of Pern* contains a series of short stories including one that precedes the colonization of the planet and focuses on the Survey team, the first humans to encounter Pern. Other stories deal with various aspects of Pern history, including the founding of new Holds and Weyrs and a rescue team from the Federation. *The Dolphins of Pern* details the intelligence of the dolphins, who also colonized Pern when the humans did. This novel explores the resumption of a special relationship between the dolphins and the humans. Over 2,525 years of Pern's history appear in *The Dragonriders of Pern*.

The last five books bring the series to a chronological and thematic close. *Dragonsdawn* explores the history, the trials, and the triumphs of the first settlers of Pern. *The Renegades of Pern* covers the same period as the *Harper Hall Trilogy* but explores Pern through the perspective of a trader, rather than from that of a member of a Hold, Weyr, or Craft. At the same time that Lessa, the heroine of *Dragonflight*, resists Fax and Impresses a queen dragon, another woman, Thella, rebels against the strictures of Hold life for a female and creates a band of criminals. Thella's cruel and villainous behavior reveals that both highly positive and negative roles are available to women on Pern. In *The Dragonriders of Pern*, 9 of the 13 books focus on female characters, two eponoymously, *Moreta* and *Nerilka's Story*. In many of the novels, but especially *Moreta*, *Nerilka's Story*, *Dragonsong* and *Dragonflight*, female protagonists face genuine hardships because of their society's sexism. Furthermore, the extraordinary women such as Menolly (*Dragonsinger*), Lessa (*Dragonflight*), and even the archvillain Thella (*The Renegades of Pern*), explicitly comment on the inequality of gender roles.

The Chronicles of Pern provides the planet's prehistory and fills in gaps in the development of Pern Holds and Weyrs. By the end of *All the Weyrs of Pern*, the discovery of a computer forever changes the Pernese cycle of Threadfall; the Pernese begin to recover the technology, some of it lost by the original settlers and some merely lost through the passage of time. Jaxom, his white dragon Ruth, and other characters from the *Harper Hall Trilogy* figure prominently in this story, providing another aspect of closure to the series. Like *The Renegades of Pern* and the *Harper Hall Trilogy*, *All the Weyrs of Pern* and *The Dolphins of Pern* cover an approximately parallel time, but from very different perspectives. While the computer Aivas dominates the events of *All the Weyrs of Pern*, in *The Dolphins of Pern*, the computer and the changes in Pern society are viewed from a distance. Instead, McCaffrey provides the dolphins' perspective, and that of a dragonrider and young boy who love the dolphins very much. This emphasis on the nonhuman creatures provides a new slant to life on Pern, because while the dolphins have a close relationship with humans and have also been like the dragons altered by the drug mentasynth, to be telepathic, the dolphins are more independent and autonomous than the dragons. With *The Dolphins of Pern*, McCaffrey covers the earth, air, and sea of Pern. Each part of the world has its own unique culture, yet all are interdependent to a degree. Part of the appeal of the series is the perceptive and carefully sketched relationships between different societies.

Because there are so many novels in this series, we cannot consider them all closely here. Instead, this chapter will focus on readings of the *Harper Hall Trilogy* (*Dragonsong*, *Dragonsinger*, *Dragondrums*); *Moreta: Dragonlady of Pern*; *All the Weyrs of Pern*, and *The Dolphins of Pern*, with appropriate reference to the other seven books. These texts reveal the major themes and issues in *The Dragonriders of Pern* series: the figure of the outsider, character development and maturation, and the necessity of social and individual change and flexibility. *The Dragonriders* series reveals McCaffrey's belief that the ability to adapt and change is necessary, both for individuals and for societies. The ability to initiate or accept innovation separates her heroes from the villains throughout the series.

CHARACTER DEVELOPMENT

The Outsider

Like *Dragonflight*, the first installment of *The Dragonriders of Pern*, the novels in *The Harper Hall Trilogy* focus on a young protagonist. The focus on the gradual acclimation and recognition of special talents provides the perspective that shapes all of *The Dragonriders* novels. *Dragonflight*'s heroine, Lessa, begins the series struggling to regain her Hold from a usurper named Fax, who has killed the rest of her family. Less than 20 Turns (years) old, Lessa has been fighting since she was a young girl. Her determination, resilience, and special telepathic skills enable her to wage a successful battle against a formidable foe—the usurper Fax. He has taken over not only her family's Hold, Ruatha, but also six other Holds. While *Dragonflight* is narrated in the third person and alternates between Lessa's and her lover's point of view, the novel pushes the reader to identify with Lessa's perspective. McCaffrey sympathetically presents Lessa's frustrations and struggles. This sympathy for a young adolescent hero or heroine who has not yet found his or her niche in the world appears prominently in the *Harper Hall Trilogy* and throughout the *The Dragonriders of Pern*. In several novels, an alienated young adult finds the courage to develop special skills and to help Pern, and in so doing, finds a place in society.

Through her portraits of these young people, McCaffrey foregrounds the special skills of those whom others overlook. She lets her readers know that a lonely outcast may have a special talent or skill that only needs persistence and faith to develop. In *Dragonsong*, for example, we see the world from Menolly's point of view. She is the daughter of a Lord of a Sea-Hold, a gruff man who cares primarily for fishing and boats, and who doesn't think much of girls or music. While Menolly's great gifts are recognized by the Hold's Harper, he teaches her in private because of the belief that only males are Harpers. Menolly's misery stems from her inability to develop her great musical talent, denied her because of her gender. From her grief and her cruel mistreatment by her family, we see how wrong it is to deny anyone the opportunity to develop her skills, simply because of custom.

Two critics have focused on Menolly and discussed her significance. Anne Cranny-Francis, for example, singles out Menolly for analysis in a chapter on feminist science fiction. Cranny-Francis praises the way that McCaffrey has Menolly defeat the system that says she cannot be a Harper because she is female, and emphasizes the importance of Menolly as a Harper who can now subvert the patriarchal ideology encoded in ballads (53). However, Cranny-Francis also points out that in a ballad about Menolly's own impression of fire lizards, she depicts herself as male, and that in many ways Menolly functions as an honorary male; that is, a woman who adopts a male persona and does not ask the system to change in any way except to allow her into the system (70). But Cranny-Francis does acknowledge that while *Dragonsinger* is not a radical feminist text, it does contain feminist elements. Cranny-Francis suggests that McCaffrey's position is "a useful compromise given the size of the audience she therefore reaches" (71). Marleen Barr goes even further and argues that in *Dragonsong*, McCaffrey "critiques master narratives about female artists' inferiority" (11–12). Barr cleverly points out that even the main character's name points to this issue: "men-only" (31).

Similarly, in *Dragonsinger* we see Menolly adapt to being in Harper Hall, where she must still face jealousy and cruelty because she is different from the other girls, none of whom are being trained as Harpers. However, Menolly also finds friends and develops her musical talents. Her young friend Piemur provides the focus for *Dragondrums*, in which he must deal with his voice changing and develop other skills—in particular, drumming. Piemur also faces ostracism because of his excellence in drumming and even confronts death when his fellow apprentices grease the stairs and cause him to fall and seriously injure himself. From the first heroine, Lessa, to the most recent heroes, Jaxom (*The White Dragon, All the Weyrs of Pern*) and Readis (*The Dolphins of Pern*), McCaffrey emphasizes the narrative point of view of the gifted outsider. Jaxom is the son of Fax, who took over Lessa's Hold, but like Lessa, he is an outsider. His mother dies at his birth, and his father falls in a duel with a dragonrider at almost the same moment. Jaxom further separates himself from others when he Impresses a white runt dragon. As the heir to Ruatha Hold, Jaxom has no business becoming a dragonrider. He is not officially on the Hatching Ground, where the dragon eggs warm and then hatch, and he helps Ruth, his dragon, break free from his shell, another aberration. Dragons are supposed to break out of their shells by themselves. Ruth's diminutive size and odd color—there are no other white dragons—cause some to view him as an abomination. In *All the Weyrs of Pern*, another dragonrider tries to kill Jaxom and describes Jaxom and Ruth as "Unnatural man, unnatural dragon!" (304). Like Menolly, Ruth has special abilities that later prove crucial to saving Pern; alone among the dragons, Ruth knows where he is in time. Ruth's unique ability to understand chronology eventually saves the planet.

The criticism of Jaxom and Ruth and their special place in Pern society supports again McCaffrey's recurrent theme that the outsider and the ostracized can offer something very special to society. McCaffrey demonstrates again that treating someone badly because he or she is different is not only unkind, but also unwise. As the only Lord of a Hold to

Impress a dragon, Jaxom brings together two different groups of Pernese. Similarly, Readis, the young heir to the newly founded Paradise River Hold, breaks tradition through his relationship with dolphins. Readis is also separated from other young people by his withered leg, a crippling that occurred from a sea-thorn. His mother exacts a promise from Readis that he will not seek out the dolphins, but by the end of the narrative Readis strikes out on his own, as Menolly had done. Like Menolly, Readis is rewarded for his initiative. Becoming the first dolphineer in centuries, Readis works with a dolphin and founds a new Craft Hall, Dolphin Hall. Through characters such as the young Lessa, Menolly, Jaxom, and Readis, McCaffrey's readers are encouraged to identify with and champion the success of an underdog. In these characters, readers find adolescent characters who have great potential, and we have the pleasure of following them as they mature and realize that potential.

The Dolphins of Pern also contains another version of this narrative emphasis on the outsider. Through italicized sections, we are privy to the dolphins' thoughts and perspectives. While the other books in the series provide brief examples of dragon thought (also signaled by italics), *The Dolphins of Pern* opens with a prologue in which dolphins vainly try to signal humans through a bell. The prologue thus sets the tone of dolphins yearning and endeavoring to initiate contact with humans, but they must wait thousands of years until a young perceptive human male (Readis) realizes the dolphins' intentions. This novel's emphasis on non-human characters continues throughout the book. The special sonar capabilities of the dolphins enable them to diagnose illnesses and pregnancy. Some humans resent and refuse to believe that dolphins are sentient and that they can actually offer humans assistance, but after the dolphins help many humans even Radis's mother accepts their value. By emphasizing what the dolphins have to offer humans, McCaffrey reiterates her theme of the value of the outsider, of those who are different—even those so different that they are not even human!

Moreta: Dragonlady of Pern differs from the novels that focus on young heroes or heroines set in Pern's present, thousands of years after the original settlement. *Moreta* presents a pecular narrative challenge because the reader already knows Moreta's fate from the other books in the series. "The Ballad of Moreta" is referred to in both *Dragonflight* (19, 92, 282) and *Dragonsinger* (119). By traveling on dragons and carrying vaccine to infected Holds, Moreta proves she is a heroine because she rescues her planet from a disease. Tragically, an exhausted Moreta goes "*between*," the place where dragon and dragonrider go to fly quickly from place to place, but Moreta and the dragon both die. Fleshing out the ballad presents McCaffrey with the challenge of getting her readers to identify and sympathize with a doomed character.

Unlike *Dragonflight*, *The Harper Hall Trilogy*, *The White Dragon*, and *Nerilka's Story*, but similar to *Dragonquest*, *Moreta* focuses on a fully mature adult protagonist. Moreta has already been a dragonrider for 20 Turns (years). A bit restless and dissatisfied with her human mate, Moreta enjoys herself at a Gather, a Hold festival that brings Pernese from all over to trade and congregate. We identify and sympathize with Moreta's attraction for Alessan, Lord of Ruatha, and his pleasure in Moreta's beauty and verve. The readers' interest in their pleasure is all the more intense with the knowledge that plague is about to strike Pern. In *Moreta*, McCaffrey takes the challenge posed in the Introduction to *Dragonflight* by depicting a legend before she becomes a legend. By showing Moreta as a real, compelling, believable human being with loves and lusts and problems, McCaffrey connects the struggles of current-day Pernese to those of their forbears. As a writer, McCaffrey also deftly develops a plot from a brief story and ballad from her other Pern books. Through the character of Moreta, McCaffrey shows how a historical figure may not be quite as perfect as she is depicted in history.

To a lesser degree, McCaffrey similarly develops Jim Tillek in "The Dolphin's Bell" from *The Chronicles of Pern*. Tillek has a Hold named after him, and the leader of all the dolphins is always known as "the Tillek," reflecting Jim Tillek's preeminent position among humans and dolphins of Pern. However, in "The Dolphin's Bell" the reader encounters a very human Jim Tillek managing the evacuation of the Landing after a volcanic eruption and falling in love with a dolphineer. This story, like *Moreta*, brings a historical figure vividly to life. Through "The Dolphin's Bell," "The Survey Pern (c)," (*The Chronicles of Pern*), a story that depicts the survey team and explains why they missed the dangers of Thread, and *Moreta*, McCaffrey suggests that history inevitably distorts and dehumanizes our predecessors.

Character Change

Part of the underdog's appeal in *The Dragonriders of Pern* series is that the underdog grows dramatically over the course of the novel. To discover their skills, the characters must grow in wisdom and maturity; they must persevere over incredible odds. Their character development is inevitably enhanced by the dragons. Mary T. Brizzi (*The Dragonriders of Pern*) notices this quality in Lessa and Mirrim, (a major character throughout), who both minimize their bad tempers after they bond with dragons (*Anne McCaffrey* 41). Because dragons are telepathic, they see deeply into human character. They "Impress" or choose a human to bond with when they are only seconds out of their eggs. While the dragons are usually constrained to choose someone of their own sex, the dragons choose from a variety of applicants on the Hatching Ground, and occasionally they choose someone not on the ground, but in the stands. Being chosen by a dragon signifies that a human has some special qualities and potentials. In fact those who are chosen to be on the Hatching Ground have already passed rigorous scrutiny by the highly sensitive and perceptive dragons. Dragons are wise, common-sensical, and passionate, and with a few exceptions, these qualities are shared and enhanced in the dragonrider, as the dragon and its human share everything. When a human dies, its dragon inevitably goes *between*, and dies too. Except in a few cases, a human whose dragon dies (from being badly scored by Thread, or accidentally killed by a collision or another dragon's phosphine emission, for example) also dies. When the dragonrider lives on without his or her dragon, the person is usually considered crippled, as Lytol is in *Dragonflight* or as Giron is in *The Renegades of Pern*. A dragonless man is an object of pity, and he carries the mark on his loss visibly. Lytol, for example, has "eyes, sick with a hungry yearning" (*Dragonflight*, 17). After his encounter with Lytol, F'nor, another dragonrider, "murmurs pityingly, 'To be dragonless'" (21). His half-brother F'lar, also a dragonrider, is equally moved and they have a hard time speaking because Lytol's plight has so affected them. Dragonless riders are rare, but even one reminds the other dragonriders that the great attachment they have with their dragons would make their loss almost unbearable. McCaffrey presents this lifelong relationship of telepathic communication and devotion as universally envied; those who can never hope to Impress a dragon desire to Impress a fire lizard, to have even a greatly diminished version of the dragon/dragonrider relationship. This diminution and imitation are carried even further by McCaffrey's fans, many of whom appear at science fiction conventions with stuffed dragons on their shoulders (Brizzi, *Anne McCaffrey* 39). This affectation should be read as a tribute to the power of McCaffrey's imagination.

Because of the unique and powerful bond dragons have with their riders, dragons strongly influence the maturation of their riders. The relationship with the dragon is the most intimate and compelling relationship possible. Humans and dragons share everything—every experience and emotion. To be chosen by a dragon not only provides a human with prestige, but also, much more importantly, provides the human with an all-encompassing and unconditional love. At the same time, this love is strengthened by the responsibility that dragon and rider share of combating Thread. This mycorrhyzoid spore periodically falls upon Pern, consuming all organic matter it contacts. Thread is destroyed most quickly and safely in the air, by a dragon's emission of phosphine, produced by eating firestone. In the beginning of the series, it is only dragonriders who experience this unique relationship. In *Dragonflight*, Lessa's life changes forever when her queen chooses her, and other dragonriders, too, become stronger and wiser from their relationship with these alien creatures.

But by the writing of the *Harper Hall Trilogy*, another possibility exists: the Impression of a fire lizard (in accordance with their size and smaller stature, no capitals are used to describe activities that are always capitalized for dragons, Brizzi, *Anne McCaffrey* 43). Much smaller, and the creatures from which dragons were bred originally, fire lizards also bond and communicate telepathically with a few humans. Discovering and caring for fire lizards makes Menolly a stronger and a wiser person. In *Dragonsinger*, she rescues a clutch of fire lizard eggs and impresses nine fire lizards. She teaches them to sing, thus presaging her new role as Harper. As we learn from all the novels in the series, a Harper has a much more important job than that of an entertainer. Each Hold has a Harper, whose job it is to instruct the young through teaching ballads and to commemorate and preserve history through other ballads. Harpers are also deeply involved in Pern politics, and Masterharper Robinton frequently intervenes and manipulates events for the good of all Pern. Master Harper Robinton impresses a fire lizard too. In *Dragonsong*, Menolly helps others to impress fire lizards, and they discover ways to work with the fire lizards to bring messages. In *Dragondrums*, Menolly's friend Piemur Impresses a queen fire lizard, a reward for his ingenuity and cleverness. The dragon's or fire lizard's love furnishes an occasion for the protagonist to demonstrate altruism, and then to be rewarded for it. The love of a dragon or fire lizard almost always signals the worth and character development of the protagonist. Furthermore, impressing a fire lizard or a dragon signals responsibilities: to feed the rapaciously hungry animal at first, but also to care for its well being, to train a fire lizard, or to learn how to fight Thread—the last, a life-threatening adventure.

In *Moreta*, Moreta has already demonstrated her worth as a healer and as a dragonrider. Even though she is already a mature adult, she, like the young protagonists of the other *Dragonrider* novels, changes over the course of the novel. The development of her character occurs as she blossoms in her relationship with Alessan. Although their love is doomed, or perhaps because of it, they both grow. Their love is almost literally stolen from time, as they use the dragons' ability to time travel to steal a precious six hours. While McCaffrey doesn't dwell on their physical passion, the narrative emphasizes the particular beauty of their physical love, a love that positively affects those around them.

Jaxom also experiences a wise and mature love with Sharra, a healer. Over the course of *The White Dragon* and *All the Weyrs of Pern*, he develops from a gangly boy into a mature leader. With his dragon Ruth, Jaxom averts a major conflict between Oldtimers and Benden Weyr when he returns Ramoth's queen egg, stolen by the Oldtimers. Over the course of time covered by *The Dragonriders of Pern*, many protagonists move from gawky adolescence to mature adulthood, and McCaffrey depicts sexual love as a natural part of that process. Dragons help here as in all other aspects of human development. Dragonriders mate with the rider of whomever their dragon mates with—avoiding, in the cases of Lessa and F'lar in *Dragonflight* and Torene and M'Hall in "The Second Weyr" (*The Chronicles of Pern*), the awkwardness sometimes associated with new sexuality. For Torene, she experiences sexuality first through her queen's experience: "she was Alaranth more than she was Torene" ("The Second Weyr" 205), and either her dragon or M'Hall's dragon comments *"We both have what we wanted"* (209). McCaffrey presents sexuality as a quality of life that is, like all others, enhanced by having a dragon partner. If, as Brizzi argues, dragons represent "the intuitive side of the rider, the emotional, impulsive nature" *Anne McCaffrey* (38), then the importance of dragons in selecting sexual partners makes perfect sense.

PLOT DEVELOPMENT

Throughout *The Dragonriders of Pern* series, the plots focus on surviving adverse circumstances, both physical and psychological. In most cases, the plot of the novels revolves around the Impression of a dragon. The word "Impression" suggests that it is the human who does the selection, but the process is more complicated and reciprocal. Dragons and dragonriders select candidates, usually young adults, to stand on the Hatching Ground. These humans are chosen for their character and an ineluctable something sensed by the dragons. Once on the Hatching Ground, however, the humans must stand and wait for a dragon to select them. In *Dragonflight*, the Dragonrider F'lar searches for an appropriate female to Impress the queen egg that is ready to hatch; he discovers Lessa and whisks her off to a Hatching. Similar interventions structure the plot of the *Harper Hall Trilogy*. In *Dragonsong*, Menolly is rescued by a dragonrider just as she is about to be killed by Thread. In *Dragonsinger*, Menolly's talent with the fire lizards and her skill as a musician help her adapt to the strangeness of Harper Hall. Her friend Piemur finds himself threatened by Thread on the Southern Continent, and his impression of a dragon and nurturing of a baby runner, a horselike beast, enable him to survive in the most hazardous of conditions. Even the penultimate novel in the series, which focuses on a computer and technology, includes a Hatching (*All the Weyrs*).

The Dolphins of Pern, the most recent novel, briefly rehearses two brothers' experience at Hatching; a younger brother in the stands Impresses even before the brother chosen as a candidate does. Such adversities are rewarded and enabled by dragons and fire lizards, as they are in *All the Weyrs of Pern*. In this novel, Jaxom and Ruth (White Dragon), with fire lizards, enter outer space and visit the dreaded Red Star, feared as the source of the dangerous Thread. Similarly, in *The Dolphins of Pern*, Readis braves Thread alone, engages in surgery on injured dolphins when there is no available healer, and courageously swims out to meet dolphins. His work with dolphins results in the reinvention of special relationships between humans and dolphins.

In *Moreta*, the plot focuses on the struggle against a disease, which turns out to be the flu. Fighting against the plague greatly resembles the fight against Thread, in that both kill, threatening the very survival of humans on Pern. Both require dragonriders to combat their destructive powers. The Craft of Healing and the Masterhealer Capiam work against time to identify and cure the illness. While they are unable to prevent the spread of the plague, and the deaths of entire Holds, by the end of the novel they have created a vaccine, or blood serum, drawing on ancient records. It is this serum that preserves the life of Pern, as Moreta carries the vaccines to Holds where both humans and runners are immunized. Dragons play a crucial role in the plot, for they are immune to the flu, and it is through their agency that needlethorns, used as syringes, are collected from the future to administer the vaccinations. Furthermore, through the dragons' speed, the vaccine is carried to the Holds in sufficient time to prevent another outbreak. Dragons also provide the message of hope and futurity at the end of the novel. While Alessan has lost Moreta, and most of his family, his sister Oklina Impresses a queen egg, the daughter of Moreta's dragon, Orlith. So the novel concludes on a triumphant note, with Moreta's line continuing symbolically through Oklina and her queen dragon, Hannath.

The plots of the novels in this series emphasize continuation and the survival in spirit, if not body, of important characters. While there is a conventional science fiction emphasis on action and a hero or heroine, McCaffrey's plots are not unrealistic. She does frequently create characters who die, but when they do die, the reader is encouraged by the fact that the character first makes an impact on his or her society.

Theme of Innovation and Flexibility

Throughout *The Dragonriders of Pern*, McCaffrey demonstrates the importance and value of innovation and flexibility, in both individuals and society. One pattern that appears repeatedly is the necessity of resisting and changing tradition. In *Dragonflight*, Lessa defies tradition by learning how to fly her dragon back in time. By doing so, she brings forward Weyrs of Oldtimers, dragonriders and dragons from hundreds of years in the past, to help her Weyr fight Thread. Unfortunately, these same Oldtimers prove unable to cope with new customs, and in their arrogance they are exiled to eventually die out. The price of being unable or unwilling to adapt is extinction. In *Dragonsong* and *Dragonsinger*, Menolly alters tradition when she becomes a Harper, an occupation traditionally reserved for men. Through her impression of fire lizards, she also alters the fabric of Pern society by introducing a new form of human/dragon bonding. In *The White Dragon*, Jaxom alters tradition when he helps a white runt dragon to break its shell. Because of the white dragon's special powers, Jaxom's deviation from tradition is critical to forever ridding Pern of Thread. The Healers in *Moreta* save the population when they vaccinate humans and runners against the disease that is decimating the planet.

Even in terms of sexual relationships, flexibility is required. As Brizzi notes, the male riders of female dragons must mate with the male riders of the male dragons (*Anne McCaffrey* 46). Brizzi also notes that "there are also several sympathetic portraits of homosexual love, involving green dragon riders and their blue-rider lovers, or in, one case, a healer"

(*Anne McCaffrey* 50). As Jane Donawerth explains, another type of innovation and flexibility is demonstrated by Lessa and F'lar in their relationship. Donawerth describes the gradual change in F'lar as he grows out of his sadism and need to control, and in Lessa as she grows out of the fear engendered in her by her family's murder and all her years of guerrilla resistance. By refusing to be controlled by F'lar, Lessa teaches him to admire her strength and to see that she too can be a worthy leader. By following the example of their dragons' love and telepathic support, Lessa and F'lar show their fellow Pernese and the reader an alternative model of supportive heterosexual love. The equality that they develop provides a worthy model and a striking contrast to the exploitation of women by other men of Pern.

Perhaps the most tradition-breaking of all events is the acceptance of the computer Aivas by Masterharper Robinton and the Lord Holders. There are many who resist the computer's advice and the technology it proffers, but it is only by learning from the computer that Pernese can protect themselves from Thread and save lives. Similarly, Readis's willingness to see the dolphins as other than mere fish, along with the receptiveness to dolphins of others like Menolly's brother, Alemi, enables humans to work with dolphins. In every book in the series, an innovation, usually technological, appears and only evil or misguided characters reject change and cling to the ways of the past. Technological change usually brings with it social change, and only those Holds or Crafts that are flexible benefit.

Those individuals who see beyond tradition are the protagonists in the series, and McCaffrey reinforces our admiration for risk-takers and innovative thinkers by the cruelty of those who are conservative. In *Dragonsong*, for example, Menolly's father is depicted as harsh and uncaring. The beatings that Menolly endures simply for wanting to develop her talent emphasize the cruelty of those who force people into roles—in Menolly's case, a gender role of a passive girl. Similarly, in "Rescue Run" from *The Chronicles of Pern*, the original settler Kimmer, a mining engineer, dominates and terrifies the women in his family. Kimmer wants only to leave Pern, and his inability to adapt to the planet parallels his paranoia and greed. He secretly loads down the shuttle with his valuables, endangering everyone's life, and he is finally ejected into space—either through suicide or murder. His demise demonstrates the folly of inflexibility. The Oldtimers' greed corresponds to their inflexibility and autocratic behavior. They take valuables from Craft and Hold people, such as the gems that Piemur cleverly hides when he visits a mine at the same time as some Oldtimer dragonriders (*Dragondrums*). Similarly, the Lord Holder Toric's greed seems connected to his disdain for change. While several characters resist Aivas and the dolphins, Toric is the most adamant in dismissing them, to his downfall. It is the dolphins who patrol the waters and identify Toric's unauthorized ships. Misguidedly, Toric "resented talking animals: speech was a human attribute. Mammals or not, the creatures were *not* equal to humans, and there was no way he would change his mind on that score" (*The Dolphins of Pern* 247). Refusing to change his mind costs Lord Toric dearly, and he is just one of many inflexible and conservative characters who pay for their intransigence.

Ecological Themes

Another theme that runs through *The Dolphins of Pern* series is the importance of respecting and living harmoniously with the environment. Pern's settlers left Earth, in part because of its pollution. The human settlers chose Pern because it would allow them to found a low-tech, agrarian society. As McCaffrey explains in *Dragonsdawn*, the 6,000 colonists were "committed and resourceful people who had chosen to eschew the high-tech societies of Federated Sentient Planets" (4). The diverse settlers come from all the continents of Earth and include ethnic nomads, and their descendents all live a low-technology lifestyle. As we learn in *The Dolphins of Pern*, the dolphins in particular fled Earth for "the chance to inhabit clean waters of an unpolluted world and live as dolphins had before tech-nol-ogy ... had spoiled the Old Oceans of humankind" (5). While the discovery of Aivas, the computer, might seem to threaten this low-technology society, Aivas is very careful to provide the Pernese with only limited information. Furthermore, the computer shuts itself down after it guides the humans and dragons in permanently moving the menace of Thread away from Pern. In the most recent novel in the series, the humans are well aware of the danger posed by technology, and they are determined to avoid pollution. As Masterharper Robinton acknowledges that the oceans are unpolluted, he exclaims, "and they will stay that way! ... We shall not make the mistakes our forebears made on their world" (175). The great respect accorded Masterharper Robinton and his success in guiding events on Pern makes his pronouncement persuasive. He adds, "we can improve the quality of our lives and still remain within these precepts: a world that does not require as much of the sophisticated doodads and technology that so obsessed our ancestors. We'll be the better for it" (176). As befits a famous science fiction writer, McCaffrey is not opposed to technology, but in *The Dragonriders of Pern* she asks her readers to consider how and when technology is necessary, and what are the costs of technology.

Generic Conventions

McCaffrey draws heavily upon the science fiction conventions outlined in Chapter 2. As mentioned in that chapter, science fiction differentiates itself from fantasy or realistic fiction by its "cognitive estrangement" (Suvin) or "defamiliarization." The events in a science fiction novel fit what is currently known and believed scientifically, but with the difference that there is an extrapolation of the known. In *The Dragonriders of Pern*, the intelligence and capability of the dragons and the dolphins, who have also traveled to Pern as colonists, are based on ideas about animal intelligence and potential. Space travel, colonization, and genetics all exist now, just not to the degree of sophistication that McCaffrey projects. What McCaffrey depicts in *The Dragonriders of Pern* causes us to think, "What if?" What if legends were based on reality? What sort of government would be appropriate for an agrarian world? Would humans be different in an agrarian world? What is essential to human culture, so essential that it would be duplicated thousands of light years away from Earth, thousands of years in the future? Can humans develop relationships with species (or aliens) who are very different from them? These are some questions treated by the series.

As in many other works of science fiction, McCaffrey's novels bridge the gap between "The Two Cultures" (described by C. P. Snow) of science and art by showing their mutual dependency. Art is crucial to the politics and history of Pern. Through the Harpers, Pern's history, politics, and technology are partially preserved. A tapestry prompts Lessa to travel through time to seek help from Weyrs from the past in *Dragonflight*. In all the novels except *Dragonsdawn*, it is the ballads that preserve and inspire the Pernese as they learn how to fight Thread. However, art alone cannot protect the Pernese from Thread, or preserve their culture. They need the science of medicine and fire production, and finally, in *All the Weyrs of Pern*, they need computer science to defeat Thread. Significantly, even the computer they tap has a personality, a sense of humor, and a propensity for literary quotation. Through her blend of science and art, McCaffrey suggests that both are vital for the survival and growth of human society.

The Dragonriders of Pern series repeatedly reminds its readers of the scientific basis of Pern, its inhabitants, and its customs. The dragons are carefully described and their fire-breathing carefully explained as a result of their chewing a certain type of stone, firestone, so that dragons actually belch, rather than breathe fire (*Dragonflight* 199). The development of the fire lizards provides a genealogy for the dragons, who were bred from the fire lizards. Most of the novels begin with a foreword or prologue that explains the colonization of Pern. The type of star is described, as well as the spore life called Thread and the orbital cause for the Thread's appearing only every 200 years. The foreword thus provides the science fiction frame for each tale, but reminders of the science fiction frame also appear in characters' actions and discoveries. For example, in *Dragondrums*, we discover that grubs do the work combating Thread in the South (155), and that grubs were bred to this task in *Dragonsdawn*, the novel that describes the initial colonization of Pern (375). In *Dragonsdawn*, we also discover that even the telepathy enjoyed by dragonrider and dragon was a genetic enhancement induced by a chemical called "mentasynth" (322). Even the dragons' colors, weights, and sex were designed by the master geneticist, Kitti Ping, who improved upon natural instincts in the small fire lizards (319). Verisimilitude (reflecting reality) also appears in the well-detailed maps that appear on the frontpiece of each novel. While conditions on Pern may seem primitive from the perspective of Earth at the end of the twentieth century, the framing of colonization and subsequent abandonment of the colonists explain their feudal and nontechnological society. However, in their clever and sophisticated use of native life forms, especially the dragons, the Pernese are far ahead of our society. McCaffrey draws upon the "soft" science fiction conventions, in which mental powers rival or replace those functions fulfilled in our society by machines. Her novels thus challenge our assumptions about the place and utility of machines. The Pernese adaptation to their environment suggests that a more successful and pleasant relationship could be had with our own planet if we adopted a more ecologically based approach.

Moreta particularly emphasizes the scientific basis of the series, for its plot focuses on the struggle to find a cure for a disease. The Masterhealer Capiam employs the scientific method of experimentation with drugs, and a careful etiology (study of the cause) of the disease and its symptoms. He searches his Craft records to find evidence and information about previous examples of disease. The real hero of the novel is science; Moreta is its handmaid, as a healer herself. The novel's moral is to maintain records and to use scientific methods. Without them, Pern would have been decimated by the disease. Human complacency and arrogance are also criticized, especially the Holders who doubt the effectiveness of science and healers. But art plays a crucial role too. The music and teaching ballads of the Harpers contain clues to the problems faced by the Pernese. The Harpers provide a crucial means of communication during the quarantine necessitated by the plague. In *Dragonflight*, it is a tapestry that provides the clue to the dragons' time-traveling ability. The ballads also contain critical clues about when the dreaded Thread spore will fall and how best to fight it. McCaffrey emphasizes the ways in which knowledge becomes encoded in art in the introduction to the first novel, *Dragonflight*. "When is a legend legend? Why is a myth a myth? How old and disused must a fact be for it to be relegated to the category 'Fairy-tale'?" (xi). The answer throughout *The Dragonriders of Pern* series is: Always take legend and myth seriously.

Mythological Implications

Ursula K. Le Guin describes science fiction as "the mythology of the modern world," and certainly *The Dragonriders of Pern* can be interpreted as an attempt to create a new mythology. Myths are fabulous stories that are culturally significant because they explain how things came to be in a society. Myths explain how the world was created and why people behave the way they do. Myth provides us with patterns and ways of thinking and understanding the world. Myth naturalizes and universalizes certain beliefs and ideologies, making them unquestioned and inviolate. Myth tells stories with morals and implicit guides for behavior. Myth also functions socially, to build a group of people into a cohesive and coherent society. Studying myths is important, because they provide a clue to a society's values. We may tend to think of myths as only belonging to ancient or "primitive" cultures, but all societies, including our own, use myth.

While science fiction myth does not carry the overt layers of sacredness that earlier myths have, current attitudes toward science do implicitly expect the miraculous of science, and science fiction myth does promote certain beliefs and attitudes. Science fiction myth may be equally or more powerful because it cleverly (or insidiously, depending on your beliefs) promotes myth through entertainment. We may be all the more suscep- tible to science fiction myth because it does not announce itself as pro- moting a belief system or promulgating values. Nevertheless implicit in much U.S. science fiction myth is a respect for science and progress, a belief that science can and will triumph over problems. By suggesting and showing that science provides the solutions for innumerable prob- lems on Pern, McCaffrey implants the idea that the same is or should be true of science on Earth. All these elements of myth can be identified in *The Dragonriders of Pern*.

While the very idea of dragons might seem fantastical and mythical, McCaffrey carefully provides a scientific basis for the dragons. Their cre- ation through science reifies her initial presentation of legend and myth as forgotten science. In this regard, McCaffrey reflects an interest in re- telling myth as science that structures the work of many other science fiction writers such as Frank Herbert, whose *Dune* series similarly creates a fantastic world of engineered giant worms, or Joan D. Vinge's or Andre Norton's witches, who have apparently magical powers that are actually scientifically based. These writers thus corroborate an alternative view of actual historical witches as they suggest witches and magic could be used as the basis for entire worlds.

In *The Dragonriders of Pern*, McCaffrey follows a science fiction "law" encapsulated by another famous science fiction writer, Arthur C. Clarke: "Any sufficiently advanced technology is indistinguishable from magic" (Pournelle 245). McCaffrey uses the advanced technology of the dragons to present us with a society that does not question its assumptions. Re- peatedly, the Pernese find themselves in trouble for letting their knowl- edge turn into legend that is then disregarded or dismissed. When Thread doesn't fall for 400 turns, they become complacent and lapse in their vigilance against greenery and Hold maintenance. It is only because F'lar, a dragonrider, understands the importance of the ballads and sto- ries that Pern survives when Thread finally and inevitably does fall. The cohesion among Hold, Craft, and Weyr also begins to deteriorate, and again it is the myths that explain why each group has certain sacred, inviolable functions. *The Dragonriders of Pern* shows that disregarding myth, or trying to maintain a culture without myth, will inevitably fail. Myth not only provides cohesion, but also insights for future develop- ment. On Pern, there have long been stories that dragons were de- scended from fire lizards, but it is only when young adults take these stories seriously that fire lizards are finally impressed and tamed into assets for Pern society. Finally, it is myth and ballad that redeem individuals and provide the beleaguered Pernese with something to believe in. The courage demonstrated by Moreta enables and inspires dragon-riders centuries after her courageous feat. In her incorporation of ballads into each novel, McCaffrey both creates a sense of verisimilitude and a sense of the importance of her storytelling. The myth of a world in which humans and dragons live and work in a close bond inspires us with the hope that we too can someday work more closely with nature. The bliss and harmony experienced by the dragonriders give McCaffrey's readers a reason to believe and hope for a different relationship between humans and nature, humans and animals. In the combination of science and magic through the figure of the telepathic dragon, McCaffrey draws on our own society's belief in science, but modifies it to a nonmechanical science.

Dragons have been a part of many myth-making systems, and their symbolism is both terrifying and inspiring. For example, in Chinese culture, dragons are fierce and terrifying creatures associated with the emperor. St. George fought the dragon, clearly signifying its evil, and numerous depictions of dragons have them eating princesses or greedily amassing treasure, as in *Beowulf* or *The Lord of the Rings*. However, McCaffrey's dragons do much more than resurrect a figure from fairy tales and ancient myths. McCaffrey's dragons help define good and evil in a society and in individuals. The stories about dragons, as well as the dragons themselves, help the society undergo change. Through the dragons, McCaffrey helps us to examine our own society for the ways that it treats or abuses nature. The pastoral beauty of Pern and its inhabitants' happiness point toward an Edenic world, one in which individuals do have the power to make a difference. The myth of Pern provides an alternative to the power-mongering myths of the ancient world, and also an alternative to another "myth"—that of capitalism. Looking at *The Dragonriders of Pern* through a Marxist lens reveals that there is another way to read McCaffrey's series.

A MARXIST READING

A Marxist approach to *The Dragonriders of Pern* would examine the structures of power and commercialism. Karl Marx's writings emphasize a social evolution based on economic differences and conflict between classes of people: the working class, the bourgeoisie or middle class, and the ruling class. A Marxist view of the world stresses the ways that the wealthy exploit and dehumanize the working class. Karl Marx described capitalism as a corrupt class system in which only those who owned the means of production exercised any actual political or economic power. Writing in the mid-nineteenth century, Marx believed that soon the working class would rise up against the middle and ruling classes. This revolution never occurred in the way that Marx envisioned it, but his ideas have helped historians and literary critics analyze culture. Literary Marxism examines the ways in which writers reflect aspects of the class struggle based on economic differences.

A Marxist approach might emphasize McCaffrey's writings in terms of their position as bestsellers, as material objects that have a particular function in a particular historical period. Books, like other parts of culture, contain "ideology," or a set of cultural beliefs. A Marxist could analyze *The Dragonriders of Pern* series to see what it reveals about economic and other attitudes. While less pronounced in *The Dragonriders of Pern* than in her other novels, McCaffrey displays a keen interest in economic considerations, and in her construction of societies on other worlds she always takes account of economic incentives and effects on events.

Pern's economic system is feudal, a step before capitalism in which a lord owned land and people worked for him without any hope of advancement. The Holds, Crafts, and Weyrs are hierarchical, with a Master or Lord at the head of each. Because Pern is primarily preindustrial, the reader has an opportunity to examine a world as yet uncorrupted, or only beginning to be corrupted by capitalism. There is very little that could be described as private enterprise on Pern except the Traders, which are introduced in *The Renegades of Pern*, and the main character Jayge, who soon abandons trading and eventually becomes part of his own Hold. The Holds produce agriculture, the Crafts make products, and the Weyrs provide protection. In this system, each group is dependent upon the other. This system of mutual dependency is in many ways ideal. Of course, the Holds sometimes see the Weyrs as parasitic, especially in the 200 Turns between Threadfall. The Crafts must wrestle with the loss of knowledge endemic to a guild system; some guild leaders die before passing on their secrets. But while there are problems on Pern, the problems are not caused by class conflicts or separation. There is very little mobility among Holds, Crafts, and Weyrs, but the novels focus on the notion of innate quality when dragons search for candidates to Impress the hatching dragons. This hope of mobility does much to obviate the inflexibility of the groups, especially as the novels frequently focus on a character who moves from one group to another, such as Menolly (*Dragonsong, Dragonsinger*) who against all odds becomes a journeyman Harper because of her talent, and who also impresses nine fire lizards.

A Marxist approach to the series would emphasize the romanticization of feudalism and point out the ways that the class system is reified in the novels. For example, there are numerous references to characters referred to only as "drudges." Lacking identity, these characters exist almost as automatons, functional and without any character or depth. Little empathy is shown in the narratives for these characters, who seem almost to be unhuman or subhuman. For example, in *The Renegades of Pern*, Lady Thella's father chastises her not for beating a drudge to death but for killing a runner beast. In *All the Weyrs of Pern*, a stupid drudge who is involved in the plot to abduct the Masterharper is rewarded for her slowness and ignorance with a job; her weakness is seen as qualifying her for the position of drudge (356). The dragonriders' unquestioning acceptance of a class system and a rigid system of patriarchal inheritance typifies what Marx and Friedrich Engels wrote about the family and the feudal state. They saw a historical development from a patriarchal, male-dominated feudal system to an eventual rebellion of the working classes. Engels in particular identifies women's oppression as stemming from the rigid class structure and the patriarchal family as an economic unit.

The trader Jayge's emergence from the position of trader to land holder also repeats the myth of individual acquisition. *The Dragonriders of Pern*'s endorsement through plot and narrative approach of feudal class system would make this novel problematic for a Marxist reader. *The Dragonriders of Pern* could be criticized for endorsing romantic myths crucial to capitalism of individual achievement. If you are encouraged to believe that exceptional individuals will rise to the top of a society, then there is no need for widespread social change. Marxist literary criticism tends to privilege the realistic novel over science fiction because realistic texts more clearly and directly expose the problems of a class system.

5

Brain Ship Series and *Crystal Singer* Series

While Anne McCaffrey's other series do not contain as many books or cover as long a period as *The Dragonriders of Pern* series, the *Brain Ship* series and the *Crystal Singer* series contain original contributions to the genre of science fiction. Both the *Brain Ship* and *Crystal Singer* novels depict engaging and temperamental heroines coping with unique physical alterations to their bodies and the concomitant strengths and weaknesses their conditions present. The heroines' physical alterations force the reader to consider what it means to be human: Do we define humanity by our bodies, or can our bodies be drastically altered and the beings remain human? These are important questions that computer scientists grapple with in the fields of artificial intelligence and robotics. McCaffrey addresses these questions through two original creations—brain ships and crystal singers—that allow McCaffrey to experiment with a wide range of settings and plots involving the unusual skills of these breeds. The unique qualities of brain ships and crystal singers also enable McCaffrey to explore recurrent themes: the definition of humanity, the importance of art to individual humans and to human society, the value of the outsider, and gender differences.

SERIES DEVELOPMENT

In the *Brain Ship* series the protagonists are "shell people," characters who because of physical deformities are condemned to die unless their parents decide to "permit it to become an encapsulated 'brain,' a guiding mechanism in any one of a number of curious professions" (*Ship Who Sang* 1). This rather dry description provides little hint of the extraordinarily vivid personalities that brain ships display in the series. "Brains suffer no pain, live a comfortable existence in a metal shell for several centuries, performing unusual service for Central Worlds" (1). Set apart from other humans, brains nevertheless display uniquely human qualities such as love and self-sacrifice. Similarly, in the *Crystal Singer* series, crystal singers provide invaluable services to Federated Sentient Planets, the same organization of planets that provides the setting for Mc-Caffrey's *Rowan* series (see Chapter 6). Because they have perfect pitch and can sing, crystal singers are uniquely suited to absorb a symbiont, an organism that lives in close association with another organism to the advantage of both, and this enables them to "sing" to crystal. Highly valued, only the planet Ballybran's crystal enables instantaneous communication between planets and ships. Brain ships and crystal singers occupy the same universe; the events of the first *Brain Ship* book, *The Ship Who Sang*, occur several hundred years before the events in *Crystal Line*, the most recent crystal singer novel. In *Crystal Line*, a brain ship develops an affinity for crystal singers, a bonding that underscores their similarity. Like brain ships, crystal singers are depicted as a species distinctly apart from other humans—they are bound to the planet Ballybran, have remarkable physical powers including a lifespan of several centuries, but the inhabitants of other planets do not regard them as human.

While there are striking and important similarities between brain ships and crystal singers, the series develop very differently. The *Brain Ship* series begins with *The Ship Who Sang*, a series of connected short stories about Helva, a brain ship. While five of the six stories originally appeared separately, the collected stories can be read as a novel. *The Ship Who Sang* is considered as a novel in this chapter. In addition, a seventh story, "Honeymoon," concludes Helva's narrative but appears in *Get Off the Unicorn*, a collection of various McCaffrey stories. "Honeymoon" is discussed here as the final chapter in Helva's saga.

The other novels in *The Brain Ship* series are all collaborations by

McCaffrey and other science fiction writers. This method of writing raises important and interesting questions about authorship. As discussed in Chapter 2, such collaborative efforts are becoming increasingly common in science fiction, especially among women writers. In this instance, as with Andre Norton, another famous and popular science fiction writer, McCaffrey lends her stature as a well-known writer. In each case, her name appears first on the books, as is only appropriate for it is her setting and original creation of brain ships that provides the foundation for the other books. Throughout, McCaffrey remains the constant coauthor, crafting each book in the series with a different coauthor. The subsequent novels, which all feature protagonists other than Helva, are *PartnerShip* written with Margaret Ball, *The Ship Who Searched* written with Mercedes Lackey, *The City Who Fought* written with S. M. Stirling, and *The Ship Who Won* written with Jody Lynn Nye.

In contrast to the diversity of authorship and protagonists in *The Brain Ship* series, McCaffrey writes *The Crystal Singer* series by herself, and each novel focuses on Killashandra Ree, a remarkable and engaging crystal singer. *The Crystal Singer* series, which includes *Crystal Singer, Killashandra*, and *Crystal Line*, follows Killashandra from her discovery of crystal singing through her amorous adventures and her eventual triumph over the limitations of crystal singing. Along the way, Killashandra takes lovers and encounters many adventures. Her tempestuous life provides another strong female heroine for McCaffrey's readers to identify with. Killashandra and Helva, the first heroine of the brain ship series, share many characteristics that help us understand McCaffrey's themes and interests.

CHARACTER DEVELOPMENT

Helva, the heroine of *The Ship Who Sang*, and Killashandra, the heroine of *The Crystal Singer* books, have much in common despite their dramatically different bodies. Both characters struggle to overcome their limitations and to appreciate fully the strengths of their unique physical forms. Because Helva's mind controls a space ship, she has extraordinary powers and virtual immortality and impregnability. Encased in a titanium hull, her aging process slowed by the chemicals she ingests and protected by the ship's metal, Helva can potentially live for several hundred years. Similarly, because of her perfect synthesis with the Ballybran symbiont, Killashandra lives for centuries and has incredible resistance to injury and illness, including remarkable healing powers. These heroines' virtual invincibility allows them to savor extraordinary experiences that would kill normal humans. They are gifted not only with physical prowess, but also financial acumen. The heroines both handle their finances wisely.

Because of their physical capabilities and their financial acumen, both Helva and Killashandra clear their debt for their apprenticeship in their founding organizations (Central Worlds for Helva, the Crystal Singer Guild for Killashandra) in record time. Their success in freeing themselves from debt and thus from control by their bosses is one of their admirable traits. Both are exceptional members of their subgroup; Helva becomes a famous and ground-breaking brain ship, and Killashandra becomes the premier crystal singer. The characters also suffer similar problems. Helva struggles to find a companion and love while she is encased in titanium and cannot express her love physically or conventionally. Similarly, Killashandra tries to maintain satisfactory love and friendships, but she is hindered by a crystal singer's inability to remember. Their search for love is sometimes thwarted, but eventually rewarded, suggesting to McCaffrey's readers that patience and hope are the proper response to loneliness and alienation.

Both Helva and Killashandra are repeatedly compared to actresses and performers. McCaffrey uses this parallel deftly and consistently to emphasize the importance of art to the human soul. In their key interventions in human, and especially human-alien encounters, McCaffrey implies that it is artistic skills and sensitivity that will save the human race from destruction. Alien interventions also produce Helva's and Killashandra's transformation into characters who further escape the limitations of their superpowers. Helva's and Killashandra's openness with other life forms provides substantial benefits, as aliens help both escape the limitations of their physical bodies.

This pairing of Helva and Killashandra shows that Killashandra and the planet Ballybran are not as cold and forbidding as critic Mary Brizzi suggests in her chapter on "Killashandra of Ballybran" (*Anne McCaffrey*). McCaffrey has added two novels to Killashandra's saga since Brizzi's 1986 criticism, and the second two novels are more optimistic and energetic; Killashandra discovers her love, Lars, and overcomes some of the problems of crystal singing. In revising her work, McCaffrey has reduced many of the elements of evil that Brizzi finds in *The Crystal Singer* stories. Brizzi's discussion of Irish names and the diabolic in *Crystal Singer* (*Anne McCaffrey*) is persuasive, but by neglecting the importance of music, and the parallels between Killashandra and McCaffrey herself, Brizzi misses the central importance of art, especially singing's redeeming and heart-warming qualities.

BRAIN SHIP SERIES

Anne McCaffrey has identified *The Ship Who Sang* as "her favorite novel" (Brizzi 19) and "The Ship Who Sang" as "her favorite story" (*Get Off the Unicorn* 265). She also explains, "I have often called Helva [the protagonist of *The Ship Who Sang*] my alter ego" (265). Such a strong statement of identification with a character deserves exploration. There are some obvious similarities between Helva and McCaffrey. Like Helva, McCaffrey was an actress, singer and performer. Helva is strong, admirable, and powerful, like her creator. The novel is dedicated to Mc-Caffrey's father, "*to the memory of the Colonel, my father*, George Herbert McCaffrey, *citizen soldier patriot* for whom the ship first sang." McCaffrey herself explains that she wrote the first story "in an unconscious attempt to ease my grief over the death of my father, the Colonel" (*Get off the Unicorn* 265). The story stresses the power of art, an important theme in *The Ship Who Sang*, and McCaffrey transforms her grief into a moving fiction. That the first story sprang from so powerful a source may be one of the reasons that *The Ship Who Sang* has attracted so much critical attention. McCaffrey writes, "I still cannot reread it without weeping," (*Get Off the Unicorn* 265), and readers today still find the book entrancing and moving.

In 1986, Brizzi described *The Ship Who Sang* as the book of McCaffrey's "that has been the subject of the most serious critical comment" (Brizzi, *Anne McCaffrey* 19). Brizzi explains the novel's preeminence by explaining that "*The Ship Who Sang*, with its sequel 'Honeymoon,' is a gem among McCaffrey's works for its originality of concept and its structure" (19). Brizzi's discussion of the book is clear and thoughtful: She responds to critics who claim that the novel isn't " 'science fictiony' " (19) enough with a detailed analysis of the use of science in the book (20–24). (The discussion of science fiction in Chapter 2 explains in even greater detail how and why McCaffrey works as a science fiction writer.) Brizzi also focuses on the sentimentality of the book and the unity of the stories.

The following sections explore other aspects of *The Ship Who Sang*: specifically, the appeal and effect of McCaffrey's unique and clever adaptation of the cyborg, the half-human, half-machine creation; the sig-

nificance of the use of art in the plot; the importance of gender to the
novel; and the expansion of the brain ship into a series.

A New Type of Cyborg

While there have been other depictions of cyborgs in science fiction,
such as Robocop, McCaffrey's brain ships, beginning with Helva, provide a significant adaptation to the cyborg, a being who is half human
and half machine. Helva and the other brain ships combine the two common classes of cyborg as described in *The Encyclopedia of Science Fiction*:
"Functional cyborgs are people modified mechanically to perform specific tasks" and "adaptive cyborgs are people redesigned to operate in
an alien environment" (Benson and Stephenson-Payne 290). As a ship
(and in later cases, a city), the brain has specific tasks, but also is transformed to adapt to an alien environment, such as outer space. While
cyborgs are frequently menacing or objects of pity, like Robocop, Mc-
Caffrey's cyborgs are clever, lively, and appealing characters. Feminist
theorist Donna Haraway cites Helva in an essay on cyborgs, but she
doesn't cite one of Helva's most important qualities: her acceptance of
herself and her unwillingness to change, even when offered a "normal,"
healthy female body. As Haraway argues, the cyborg can offer a new
kind of role model for readers as it transcends gender and bodily defi-
nitions.

McCaffrey's Helva differs from her predecessors in several significant
ways. First, unlike Robocop, Helva becomes a cyborg before she attains
subjectivity. While other cyborgs become cyborgs because of an injury
as adults, Helva's transformation takes place over a long period, while
she is very young. Central Worlds, the government group that creates,
trains, and employs brain ships, carefully conditions its cyborgs to accept
their transformed bodies, and inculcates optimism in them by emphasizing what they have gained rather than what they have lost (conventional human bodies). In contrast, cyborgs such as the ship in Joan D.
Vinge's "Tin Soldier," experience regret and bitterness, even psychosis,
as they struggle with the loss of the human body they grew up with.

Both the reader and Helva are reconciled to her human-machine combination because she has no alternative. On the very first page of the
book readers are informed that the infant who becomes Helva faces either becoming a brain ship or euthanasia. Her birth defects are never
specifically enumerated, but they are explicitly identified as incurable,

and her appearance is presumed to be horrible. So, becoming a brain ship provides an attractive alternative to death. Again in contrast to cyborgs such as the popular film and television hero, Robocop, Helva never loses or damages her essential humanity. From childhood, Helva remains a lively, engaging, and humorous personality. She is likeable, as the many people who travel with her discover.

What McCaffrey has done for the cyborg parallels Isaac Asimov's considerable achievement with robots. Whereas robots were generally regarded as evil and depicted as a danger to humans, after Asimov's *I, Robot*, a collection of unified short stories like *The Ship Who Sang*, robots came to be regarded as humanity's friends and allies. This new vision of robots lead to such lovable robot friends as R2D2 and C3PO in *Star Wars*, and Commander Data of *Star Trek: The Next Generation*. While cyborgs before *The Ship Who Sang* most often appeared as a danger to humans, after *The Ship Who Sang*, cyborgs more nearly resemble Donna Haraway's beneficent cyborg. Anyone who has read the *Brain Ship* series would welcome the opportunity to ride with or partner with a brain ship.

The special relationship that Helva and other brain ships have with their human partners, or brawns, is another change in the depiction of the cyborg pioneered by McCaffrey. This relationship is one of special intimacy, and through many examples McCaffrey parallels the relationship to a marriage. Similar to the Impression of dragons in *The Dragonriders of Pern* series, the courtship of a brain ship is a very serious matter. In *The Ship Who Sang*, Helva experiences several courtships. The brain ships select their human partners, or brawns. The partner is called a brawn because despite the high intelligence brawns must demonstrate, their prime function is to serve as a mobile partner for the ship. After she chooses a brawn, the brain ship changes her name, her designation, so that her initials reflect the combination of the ship and brawn's names. For example, before she chooses a partner, Helva is "XH 834." After she selects Jennan, because of his careful attention to her, she becomes "JH 834" (Jennan-Helva 834). "Hers was a curious courtship—this would be only the first of a series of marriages for her, for brawns would retire after 75 years of service, or earlier if they were unlucky. Brains, their bodies safe from any deterioration, were indestructible" (10).

Jennan's behavior underscores the nature of their relationships, because after Helva's singing becomes public knowledge, Jennan fights many brawls to defend Helva's honor and reputation. Jennan's father was also a brawn, and when Helva expresses some jealousy because of

Jennan's ability to have relationships with other women, Jennan says, "My father gave me the impression he was a lot more married to his ship, the Silvia, than to my mother" (13). After Jennan dies as he and Helva save colonists from a nova explosion, Helva "dates" other partners until she finally discovers her true love, Niall. The story that concludes Helva's narrative is entitled "Honeymoon," again paralleling the choice of a brawn with the choice of a marriage partner. Helva and Niall's triumphant love overcomes even the obstacle of their physical separation as they merge minds after their visit to the Corviki, an advanced species of aliens who lift them from their bodies. When Helva and Niall return to the ship and their bodies, they discover that they are linked telepathically and that Helva experiences all of Niall's physical sensations. Through Helva's union with Niall, she has the immortality and abilities of a space ship plus the sensations of a human body.

McCaffrey emphasizes the advantages of being a brain ship. In a witty and clever incorporation of criticism of brain ships, McCaffrey has the Society for the Preservation of the Rights of Intelligent Minorities visit Helva. Still in school, Helva occupies her time painting a perfect copy of "The Last Supper" on the head of a screw using magnified vision and miniscule tools. When one of the visitors asks what she is doing, she shows him, but then apologizes as she realizes "you people don't have adjustable vision" (4). Brain ships are indestructible, virtually immortal. Helva even meets one brain ship that is several hundred years old. Helva has tremendous powers—she can cruise the universe and see incredible and beautiful sights, such as a sun going nova, and survive unscathed. She can and does have great adventures, such as carrying hundreds of thousands of embryos to a colony planet, breaking up a drug ring, saving lives throughout Central Worlds' planets. Along with her conventional skills, Helva also learns to use her mechanical abilities to create art. When she is complimented as a child on her lovely voice, she researches and explores her own singing capabilities. Helva sings not with her vocal chords, which would limit her to one voice, but through mechanical means, enabling her to sing every part perfectly. Helva becomes known throughout Central Worlds as "the ship who sang." And while she is unique, every brain ship demonstrates unique capabilities that make the reader and other characters see them as people, rather than as machines.

The Importance of Art

That Helva's uniqueness appears through her artistic abilities under-
lies a theme that emerges in all of McCaffrey's fiction, but perhaps most
strongly in the *Brain Ship* and *Crystal Singer* series. As mentioned in
Chapter 1 and earlier in this chapter, McCaffrey herself is an artist, not
only a storyteller, but also a singer and an actress ("Retrospection" 23).
Furthermore, McCaffrey develops the union of art and science, the two
cultures discussed in Chapter 2, as most science fiction writers, especially
feminist science fiction writers, do. Where McCaffrey differs is in her
explicit and consistent depiction of the particular power of art to hu-
manize, communicate, affect, and help. These features of art appear not
only in characters such as Helva, but also in the importance of art to the
plot. Art provides the means for Helva and other brain ships to develop
their characters.

Character Development

Art not only helps Helva accept her lot as a brain ship, it also allows
her to create an identity and to communicate with other human beings.
As a part of her education, Helva receives training in the fine arts. After
she explores her singing talent, she discovers that she can sing any part—
high, low, male, female. In "The Ship Who Sang," Helva uses her singing
to express her grief at the loss of her first partner, Jennan. In "The Ship
Who Kills," Helva uses the common language of music to reach her
despondent passenger, Kira. Kira, also a musician, becomes a "Dylanist,"
a social commentator and protestor who uses music (after Bob Dylan,
the 1960 folk artist). A Dylanist, Kira explains to Helva, " 'can make so
compelling an argument with melody and words that what he wants to
say can become insinuated into the music' " (69). Helva has occasion to
prove that she can use her singing to Dylanize, to affect the inhabitants
of a planet who are threatening her passenger. In "The Ship Who Dissembled," Helva uses her voice to seduce her kidnapper into turning her
volume controls up—after he does so, Helva uses the sound of her voice
to kill him. Helva's singing thus delights other humans, expresses grief,
breaks down barriers with other human beings, influences people, and
even kills.

At the beginning of the book, Helva is compared to an actress (9). In
two of her most important missions, Helva has the opportunity to act in

Shakespeare's plays, a measure of an actor's skill. Helva's art is not only important to her, it also enables her to complete a mission vital to the advancement of the human race. Helva performs beautifully; as with her singing, she can play any role. One actor even describes her as a "bodiless Bernhardt" (a reference to the nineteenth-century actress Sarah Bernhardt) (124). And of course, she has perfect recall of the lines. When Helva is kidnapped and deprived of her sensory inputs, she manages to keep herself sane by recalling and reciting poetry to herself. Art saves her life.

Helva's skills save human lives and result in humanity's trade with an advanced alien species, the Corviki. The Corviki are technologically advanced and they offer some of their knowledge to humanity. What they want in exchange from humans is art; specifically, dramatic performances and skills. Helva carries a troupe of the finest human actors to the Corviki planet and then twice performs herself. She also practices with the troupe, helping them with lines and interpretations. In "Dramatic Mission" and "Honeymoon" Helva plies her acting abilities to entertain and educate the Corviki. As a result, the Corviki provide humanity with a new space drive and Helva becomes the first ship to be fitted with this new drive. Helva's art ensures the mission's success, and she personally benefits, and so does all humanity. Art provides a means to communicate between humans, but even more powerfully, to communicate with aliens. That the Corviki so value art suggests that humans should similarly appreciate the importance of art. Furthermore, art provides the solution to human problems as well as a valuable commodity to be traded with aliens. But perhaps the most compelling benefit of art is its transformation of Helva's limitations, her lack of a mobile, sensing human body. After the last visit to the Corviki, Helva and Niall's consciousnesses are intertwined—each sees and feels through the other. Their gift of art to the Corviki, then, results in a more perfect union of their selves. Art enables a perfect love, a conclusion supported by the choice of the Shakespearean play, *Romeo and Juliet*. However, where Shakespeare's lovers are doomed to be separated by human feuds and death, Helva and Niall are united. McCaffrey, then, shows both personal and universal reasons to endorse and support art. It benefits both individuals and humanity.

Gender

Art has associations with gender, and throughout *The Ship Who Sang*, McCaffrey uses Helva's femininity to explore differences between men and women, to the women's advantage. First, by making her first brain ship female, McCaffrey draws on a longstanding tradition of the femininity of vehicles, especially ships. While there are male brain ships, most of the brain ships in this first book are female. Because some brain-brawn relationships are same-sex, including two of Helva's, McCaffrey continues a subtle but consistent acceptance of homosexuality in her fiction. McCaffrey also parallels Helva to Cinderella, explicitly in "Honeymoon," but implicitly throughout the stories. But Helva is a feminist version of Cinderella, active rather than passive, powerful rather than a servant. McCaffrey's mention of Cinderella serves to emphasize Helva's strength and power. McCaffrey's response to Brizzi's analysis of Cinderella figures in her fiction makes her position clear: "I did NOT write the Cinderella story," McCaffrey writes. "Cinderella was a wimp, waiting for the damned prince to come find her shoe. Any gal worth her salt I know—and certainly those I write about—take the initiative and usually waylay the prince" (E-mail 3-9-95).

Helva creates strong bonds with her two female partners, Theoda and Kira. Helva's enhanced vision supports Theoda's "women's intuition" (38) about the cause and cure of a terrible plague. Helva acts as a mother to 300,000 babies whom she carries to a colony planet, a mission she jokes about, but which also has a very serious side. Helva describes herself as "a nursery ship" (62) and she also solves the dilemma about Kira's infertility problem, finding a technical solution to help Kira mother. Mothering is depicted in these stories as a noble and important task, but one that can be carried out in different ways by different women. McCaffrey depicts mothering as not only the biological act of bearing a child, but also the even more important act of nurturing. Mothering in this sense is a transition to adulthood, and Helva sees it as such: "She had passed as surely from girlhood to women's estate as any of her mobile sisters" (93). McCaffrey here valorizes a central part of femininity, as she does in many of her novels.

And if the positive depiction of Helva's femininity and its strength were not enough, in "The Ship Who Dissembled," McCaffrey provides a humorous but distressing picture of a male chauvinist and the damage he can do. Helva's partner Teron is patronizing and explicitly sexist. His inability to value her because she is female endangers both their lives; his trust of men leads to Helva's kidnapping, and it is only Helva's art and ingenuity that allow Helva to save herself, Teron, and other kidnapped brain ships. At the end of this story Helva "fires" Teron, and the reader enjoys seeing a sexist man humiliated. Gendered epithets by both Helva's enemies and friends also underscore the importance of her femininity. Several times Helva is called a witch, associating her, and her extraordinary powers, with the feminine powers of magic (see Chapter 2). Helva as "silver-plated sorceress" (43), "armored maid" (74), "Cinderella" (*Get Off the Unicorn* 282), and "tin-plated witch" (227) all suggest the combination of magic and science in the character of Helva, a triumph of feminine power.

Series Development: Coauthored Books

The *Ship* series continues in a group of novels that McCaffrey coauthors with a variety of writers. As might be expected, these books differ in approach and style; all the novels, however, remain true to McCaffrey's unique and clever creation of a human body encapsulated in a powerful machine. All of the cyborgs in the series are extraordinary and likeable, though none has quite the charm or impact of Helva.

Although Helva herself does not reappear in the subsequent books in the series all of her qualities do. *PartnerShip* is a well-written and engaging novel. McCaffrey read Ball's medieval novel about building a Gothic cathedral and "liked her attention to detail" (E-mail 4-12-95). It may be Ball's influence that explains the multitude of characters and detail in *PartnerShip*. *PartnerShip* (written with Margaret Ball) focuses on a female brain ship who struggles to find the right partner and who has adventures and escapades. Nancia, the brain ship in *PartnerShip*, has just graduated from training, and she is ready and eager to start her service as a courier ship. She takes her first journey without a brawn; alone, Nancia transports five young people, all exiled because of scandal from their influential and aptly named High Families, so called for their prestige and immense wealth. Nancia also comes from High Family stock, and she is disappointed by the corruption and evil she finds in this group of "softpersons." By the end of the novel, it becomes Nancia's task to bring the five to justice, and she does so over great obstacles. In its rough outline, *PartnerShip* follows the pattern set by Helva. Indeed, Nancia thinks of Helva as a model, acknowledging that it had become "a point of pride among shellpersons to demonstrate control over their 'voices' and all other external comm devices that Helva had shown to be possible" (2).

But where *The Ship Who Sang* centered on Helva, here McCaffrey and Ball give as much attention to the "greedy, amoral, spoiled brats" (21) who join in a pact to cause evil. The leader Polyon actually sabotages hyperchips used in prosthetics and brain ships, in a grandiose plan to control the universe. Another member of the party, Fassa, has been damaged by her father's sexual abuse; another, Alpha, is a doctor who tortures in the name of science; and a fourth, Darnell, epitomizes the corrupt industrialist. Another of the High Family passengers, Blaize, Nancia's cousin and her brawn's nephew, turns out not be evil at all, but the reader believes him to be just as evil as the others until the end of the novel. This emphasis on bleak, tortured, and torturing souls differs dramatically from the optimism that characterizes so much of McCaffrey's work. Where sex is depicted as healthy and pleasurable in most of McCaffrey's novels, *PartnerShip* reveals the dark effects of father-daughter incest. By spending so much time on these dark characters, the novel de-emphasizes the optimism that is one of the pleasures of *The Ship Who Sang*.

There are, however, glimpses of McCaffrey's vision in *PartnerShip*. A character's reaction to brain ships provides a key to his or her moral worth. Blaize's desire to be a brawn and his admiration of Nancia suggest the open-mindedness that allow him to help the aliens he is supposed to oversee. Inversely, the other four young people assume that Nancia is a drone, and the worst of them, Polyon, thinks of brain ships as "monsters" (289), when, in fact, he is the true monster. Polyon destroys the environment of the planet he oversees, another clue to his evil ruthlessness. And art again creates salvation, when Nancia's recitation of poetry keeps her sane when Polyon deprives her of sensory input. As a result of her use of poetry, Nancia foils Polyon's plans. But these elements are subdued parts of a novel that doesn't fully live up to Helva's legacy.

The Ship Who Searched, as its title's similarity to *The Ship Who Sang* suggests, comes much closer to Helva as a model. Written with Mercedes Lackey, a well-known fantasy writer who has co-written novels with Andre Norton (a famous woman science fiction writer who writes under a pseudonym), *The Ship Who Searched* contains the features that have made McCaffrey, Lackey, and Norton among the most popular writers of science fiction and fantasy. While *PartnerShip* made the brain ship only one of the characters, *The Ship Who Searched* focuses on a young girl who becomes a brain ship. We meet her at the age of seven and follow her through her successful maturation as a brain ship. Unlike *PartnerShip*, *The Ship Who Searched* adds an innovation to the series. While Helva and Nancia became shellpeople as infants, Hypatia must make the transfer at a much older age, because she has contracted a rare space plague that slowly paralyzes her. The poignancy of her situation makes the brain ship transfer more complicated for her, and for the reader.

Hypatia's name suggests her heroic role; she was "named for the first and only female librarian of the Great Library of Alexander on Terra" (12), who was killed by Christian fanatics as they stormed the library. Hypatia requires equal courage as she faces the challenge of becoming a brain ship. She contracts the paralyzing disease as she discovers an archeological site of great importance and that makes becoming a brain ship attractive to her. The only child of two famous archeologists, Hypatia, or Tia as she is known, is clever, courageous and self-sufficient. Because she has not spent much time around children her own age, Tia acts much older than her chronological age. This difference enables her to accept her illness and transformation with great fortitude; although at times, McCaffrey and Lackey movingly paint a portrait of a lonely, scared child.

Through Tia, McCaffrey can make even more obvious a point she makes about Helva: "*The Ship Who Sang* is much appreciated by the handicapped, who see in Helva the chance to surmount their problems and *be* a spaceship" (*Vision*, "Retrospection" 25). Tia's adaptation to the brain ship more nearly resembles that of an accident victim acclimating herself to a wheel chair or other technological aids. Moira, another shellperson, finds herself in a brain ship at the age of four, the only way to resist the ravages of progeria (a disease of premature aging that exists today). Tia responds to her transformation positively: waking up as a ship "was a moment that had given her back everything she had lost" (78). At her treatment center, disability is treated as something that can be overcome, and throughout, McCaffrey and Lackey show people helping each other. For example, a general, whose nephew Tia's doctor had saved, provides special permission for Tia to become a brain ship.

Like Helva, Tia finds a true love, aptly named Alexander, after the library defended by her namesake. They serve on many missions, but they are always on the alert for viruses and diseases like the one that incapacitated Tia. At one point, they rescue plague victims, a mission that requires both their skills. Ironically, Tia is protected from any contamination in her titanium column, but she rightly insists that Alexander don a space suit for protection, thus saving his life. In another mission, they work together to capture dangerous pirates, thus earning Tia a bonus and her freedom from debt and servitude to CenCom, the government that sponsers and manages shellpeople. Tia uses her money and her investments in stock to participate in an experimental cybernetic body. This body is connected to her real body and it allows her to feel and move. Like Helva, Tia uses her enhancement to express her love for Alexander. Tia thus has the best of both worlds—her brain ship abilities and virtual immortality, and a mobile feeling body. Like Helva, Tia represents a breakthrough, and the first extension and realization of her doctor's dream of all humanity benefiting from shell technology. As the doctor reminds Tia when she gets depressed, "Think of Helva. She and her brawn had a romance that still has power over the rest of known space" (146).

The reader follows Tia's development with delight, for like Helva, she is an engaging and likeable character. The focus on her struggle to adapt to being a brain ship, and the reward for her courage and perseverance evokes Helva's qualities and McCaffrey's emphasis on virtue rewarded. While art does not appear as explicitly as in *The Ship Who Sang*, the importance of archeology and archeological artifacts serves the same function. Tia's illness is almost worth the great archeological discovery of an ancient advanced space-travelling culture, and she later uses her brain ship skills to foil a scheme that uses artifacts to hide illicit drugs. The ethics of archeology are discussed at some length as important matters, and drug smuggling is presented as even more heinous when artifacts are used as cover. Most important, however, is Tia's similarity to Helva as an engaging likeable heroine with whom the reader identifies.

The City Who Fought, co-written with S. M. Stirling, focuses on a brain named Simeon who runs a station. Stirling is male, an exception to McCaffrey's practice of co-authoring with other women. McCaffrey comments that his games playing was extremely helpful in creating the novel (E-mail 3-9-95). More space opera than bildungsroman (a novel about a character's moral and psychological growth) like *The Ship Who Sang*, *The City Who Fought* nevertheless presents innovations and continues the darker vision presented in *PartnerShip*. In contrast to the younger brain ships of the earlier books, Simeon is already a mature city and he is unwilling to accept his new partner. In contrast to the emphasis on a couple in the other brain ship novels, *The City Who Fought* creates and valorizes a nuclear family, albeit a strange one, that consists of Simeon, his brawn, Channa, her lover, Amos, and an adopted 12-year-old daughter.

This focus on a small family unit separates this novel from the other brain ship books and McCaffrey's other fictions. Similarly, while space conflict does appear in the other novels, fighting occupies the center of *The City Who Fought*. A group of human refugees flees to Simeon's station, led by a brain ship of immense age who sacrifices himself to get these people to safety. Their attackers, led by the warrior Kolnari, follow the refugees and occupy the station, and a guerrilla war of resistance follows. Most of the novel depicts the bloody and brutal occupation and resistance, including the many brutal rapes and sexual collusion of women like Channa, Simeon's brawn, to lull the invaders into complacency until the Fleet Navy can arrive.

Joat, Simeon and Channa's adopted daughter, had jumped ship and lived on her own in the station for two years. Joat strikingly resembles Ridley Scott's *Aliens'* character Newt, a young girl who has a similarly androgynous name, who also hid in a station, escaping alien invaders. Like Newt, Joat is master of guerrilla tactics and she plays a pivotal role in the resistance, including the rescue of Simeon from the invaders. McCaffrey and Stirling's Joat has a similarly feminist function—showing the resilience and power of a young girl who defies traditional stereotypes of feminine weakness. Channa and another scientist, Patsy, work with Joat to save Simeon, again emphasizing the power of women when they work together. Although *The City Who Fought* is a male brain station, the novel itself focuses sharply on female characters, in keeping with the legacy of Helva and Tia.

Helva is a friend of Simeon's and he plays a recording of her wildly sensual Reticulan mating croon for Channa. Throughout the novel, as things become desperate, Simeon plays a wide range of music and reads literature to soothe Channa and Joat. For example, after they decide to adopt Joat, Simeon recites a bedtime poem to lull Channa to peaceful sleep. The next morning he starts her day off with an invigorating march. After the refugee ship almost crashes into the station, he helps her drift to sleep with soft music. Later, as Channa grapples with her love for the refugee leader, Amos, Simeon uses three recorder songs to interpret Channa's mood. While Simeon is not the accomplished performer that Helva is, he shows a sensitivity to the use of music and the power of art to heal. These are the lessons picked up and amplified in *The Crystal Singer* series.

The Ship Who Won, written with Jody Lynn Nye, is the most recent volume in *The Brain Ship* series. This novel not only repeats the series' major themes, but it also incorporates Simeon, the brain city from *The City Who Fought*. Simeon helps Carialle, a brain ship, and her brawn, Keff, escape from a bureaucrat determined to detain and study Carialle. Carialle had lost a brawn under tragic circumstances, but like Helva, Carialle is learning to cope and live and love again. Carialle and Keff discover a planet dominated by aliens with psionic powers, and it takes all of Carialle's scientific prowess and wits to protect Keff and to nego-tiate with the aliens, who are at first quite hostile.

Carialle and Keff learn the importance of language as power, and they debate the conflict between magic and science, so central to science fic-tion. Keff insists that the aliens are using magic, but Carialle insists all magic can be explained as a science. She huffily persists, "I say it's a form of energy with which I am unfamiliar" (144), and she turns out to be correct. The aliens' "magic" is an advanced science handed down to them by another race of alien beings. The planet has been almost de-stroyed by pollution and the aliens' abuse of natural resources, but Car-ialle and Keff are able to explain the danger to the aliens and persuade them to become environmentally conscious.

As in the other novels in the series, *The Ship Who Won* explores the superiority of the brain ship. Like Helva, Carialle practices art, in her case painting. And while her brawn Keff has a love affair with one of the aliens, it is Carialle whom he truly loves and calls "his Lady" (103). Keff and Carialle tell the alien female a white lie so that they can leave the planet without her. The novel ends on a comical note as Carialle and Keff realize that despite all their adventures they will still have to deal with the bureaucrat they escaped at the very beginning. *The Ship Who Won* continues the emphasis on a special relationship/romance that also shapes the plots of *The Crystal Singer* series.

THE CRYSTAL SINGER SERIES

Series Development

Crystal Singer (1982) begins the chronicle of the life and loves of Kil-lashandra Ree, a native of the planet Fuerte, whom we meet just as she has been informed by a maestro that her dream of a career as a top concert singer is over. Although Killashandra has a lovely voice and she has dedicated a decade of her life to singing, a burr or flaw mars her

voice. The reader feels the raw intensity of Killashandra's disappoint-
ment as she decides what to do next. That McCaffrey's own voice has
just such a flaw may explain why and how she can depict Killashandra's
plight so convincingly. "Though I trained as a dramatic soprano and had
both volume and range, like Killashandra, there was an unattractive burr
in my voice, which was useful for singing character parts" (*Vision*, "Retrospection" 23), but not for starring roles. Where McCaffrey found pleasure in character roles and singing with a choir, and eventually becoming
an author, Killashandra rejects the maestro's suggestion of choral work
with an emphatic, "I won't be second rank!" (*Crystal Singer* 2). As Killashandra decides to disappear, she journeys to the space port, where
she meets a mysterious man, Carrick, an encounter that changes her life
completely. Both Killashandra and Carrick hear that an approaching
shuttle emits dissonant harmonics—the ship's crystal drive is off kilter.
Carrick explains that this special sensitivity to sound is one of the crucial
qualities of a crystal singer. Killashandra has perfect pitch as well, which
will enable her to cut crystal using sound, and Carrick subtly recruits
her to be a crystal singer.

Because crystal is so vital to space travel and space communications,
members of the Heptite Guild, the guild of crystal singers, are incredibly
wealthy, mysterious, and even feared. But crystal singing has so many
dangers and side effects that Guild members are not allowed to recruit.
Before Killashandra can leave her home planet of Fuerta, its officials
insist on warning her. Killashandra's former maestro becomes hysterical,
screaming at Carrick that he is "a silicate spider paralyzing its prey, a
crystal cuckoo pushing promising fledglings from their nests" (28). Like
Helva and other brain ships, however, Killashandra is so desperate to
escape from her damaged dreams of being a concert performer that she
is willing to risk anything—even her life. Gradually, as Killashandra
moves through the Guild apprentice system, we learn more about the
dangers of crystal singing, but it is too late for Killashandra to change
her mind, and she has no one and nothing to return to.

Killashandra must be trained and undergo a grueling series of tests,
which she passes successfully. While in training she discovers that the
ability to sing crystal requires not only perfect pitch, but also the acceptance of a symbiont native to the planet of Ballybran, where crystal was
first discovered. The symbiont alters the human body, producing great
visual acumen, improvement in the sense of touch and nerve conduction,
and cell adaptation. As a result, crystal singers age extremely slowly;
they, like the brain ships, can live for hundreds of years. A crystal sin-

ger's life is extended by almost 500 years, and then recuperate quickly from injuries and have greater tolerance for extremes of heat and cold. But there are great costs to these advantages. In *The Crystal Singer* series, as in her other works, McCaffrey always shows the consequences of any change to humanity.

A crystal singer is rendered sterile by the symbiont—he or she cannot reproduce. In addition, crystal singers cannot retain their memories. They forget people and places, and they develop a strain of paranoia, which makes them unlikely to form relationships. Applicants can never leave Ballybran, and as many as one out of three develops a handicap as a result of their exposure to the symbiont, and thus cannot become crystal singers. For example, one applicant develops increased sight, which deforms his eyes, but makes him a perfect assayer for crystal. Even crystal singers cannot leave Ballybran for more than 400 days; after that time, they feel the pull of crystal and must return to the planet. In a curious evocation of vampire myths, the Guild trainer warns Killashandra's class that while crystal singers heal quickly, they cannot recover from a severed head or complete blood loss. Crystal singers, then, are a magical group of altered humans, just as brain ships are. That crystal singers are sworn never to reveal the symbiont's existence or any of their regulations makes crystal singers all the more mysterious and threatening to other humans.

Character Development

Determination and Open-mindedness Rewarded

After hearing all the deficits of crystal singing, Killashandra bravely becomes the first to breathe Ballybran's air, thus exposing herself to the symbiont. Her courage and determination are rewarded when she doesn't suffer at all through the transition. Others in her class suffer horribly, and one woman dies. McCaffrey implies that the reason Killashandra adapts so easily is because of her open-mindedness and tolerance; she wants to become a crystal singer and doesn't fear the symbiont. As with other encounters with aliens, Killashandra's with the symbiont reveals the advantages of tolerance and open-mindedness for both the individual and the species. Because of her approach, Killashandra becomes the best crystal singer, fulfilling her desire to be "top rank." At the same time, she provides Federated Sentient Planets with the black crystal that is rare and desperately needed for communications. This need shows a human face when a crew member thanks Killashandra for installing the black crystal that will enable her to speak to her mother. By overcoming her weakness (the burr in her voice) by redirecting her energy and skills, McCaffrey suggests that even when you feel that your dream has been destroyed, there will be another, even better future ahead if you are determined and open-minded.

By contrasting Killashandra's personality to that of the other hopeful crystal singers, McCaffrey shows that success requires personal sacrifice, determination, and ambition. Killashandra demonstrates all these qualities. Over time, hundreds of years, Killashandra must also cope with losing her friends to death and losing her memory, a side effect of crystal singing. All humans must adapt to change, and the way that Killashandra copes provides a model for readers. One way Killashandra adapts is to lose herself in art.

Theme of Art

Throughout *The Crystal Singer* series, McCaffrey valorizes art, explaining its importance not only to Killashandra, but also to all of humanity. The very idea of a crystal singer has embedded in it the primacy of art. Instead of "crystal technician" or "cutter," the phrase "crystal singer" evokes the practice of art, rather than a science. Crystal singing is both an art, and a science, and the crystals are used for scientific purposes. In her creation of crystal singing, McCaffrey, like the other feminist science fiction writers discussed in Chapter 2, combines art and science. The crystal singer must not only have technical skills such as the ability to cut crystal, she or he must also have the ability to sing, and the intuition to find crystal hidden in rock. Killashandra decides that singing crystal is "analogous to having the starring role in a large company. The applause could be the crystal singing in your hand, fresh from the vein, stimulating, ecstatic. The same emotional high" (252). Killashandra describes the other crystal singers as looking like "stellar performers basking in the applause of adoring audiences" (55–56). As Killashandra links the black crystal she has cut, she realizes that her work was "a solo performance if there ever was one. And she had played before the audience of an entire system. . . . She had done exactly as she had once boasted she'd do. . . . She had been the first Singer in this system" (305). As Killashandra fulfills a personal dream, she also gives the people of this system a way to communicate instantly and a safe means of communication for their mining industries.

In *Killashandra*, art's power appears in its misuse on the planet Optheria. Killashandra journeys to this planet to set the white crystal she has cut into the Optherian organ, a musical instrument with the power to affect the mood of the listeners. Despite an intense interest in music, no Optherian has ever applied to the Heptite Guild, so Killashandra has another mission—to check out the conditions on the planet. To her horror, she discovers that the planet's Elders use subliminal conditioning during their concerts, controlling the population through the guise of entertainment and uplift. Because of their conditioning, Optherians remain planet-bound and they have a high suicide rate. One clue to the evil of the Elders is their attitude toward music. They present as their own compositions the music of the great composers Bach, Beethoven, and Ravel. This blatant plagiarism disgusts Killashandra, and it suggests the Elders' complete lack of scruples. The one truly original composer on the planet, Lars Dahl, is denied an opportunity to play his music because the Elders fear original music.

Killashandra uses art to end this abuse of music and the human spirit. Cleverly Killashandra uses crystal and her voice to disrupt the Elders' monitoring device. Lars's music inspires a group of Optherians to resist subliminal control; through music Lars manifests genuine emotion and communication. Killashandra realizes that music provides a means of expression for people from other planets: "Even before this evening, Killashandra had been aware that some melodies seem to be universal. . . . Words might be changed, tempo, harmony, but the joy in listening, in joining the group singing was not: it struck deep nostalgic chords" (136). More practically, as Killashandra fights against the Elders, she discovers that "one never knows when one's early training as a singer is going to prove useful" (71). *Killashandra* repeats the lesson of *Crystal Singer* and *The Ship Who Sang*: the importance and power of art. By including an inversion, the abuse of art in *Killashandra*, McCaffrey repeats the refrain in another key, enhancing the message.

In *Crystal Line*, art enables Killashandra and other humans to communicate with a completely alien creature: sentient crystal found on a newly discovered planet. Killashandra was only in her third decade in *Killashandra*, but the third book in the series finds her in her second century. While Killashandra "wasn't much changed from the girl who had left Fuerte" (296), the universe has changed. The Heptite Guild is losing members and not replacing them, in part because they cannot recruit, and in part because perfect pitch may "be on the wane in the modern world" (237). Some change must be made to ensure the Guild's survival. One significant change occurs when Killashandra uses her ability to contact aliens on the planet Opal. The first exploration team had all died of respiratory ailments, but because of her symbiont, Killashandra should be protected from infection. Because other humans cannot speak with the alien, the Guild Master receives concessions that will help him "to reinstate the Guild to former prominence" (227); they can now advertise and recruit specialists. As "the best singer the Guild has" (133), Killashandra succeeds where others have failed; she perceives the beauty in the iridescent glow of the crystal and feeds it. She alone talks with the alien she nicknames "Big Hungry," and in an astonishing exchange, communicating with him restores her memory—all of it. Memory loss is one of the drawbacks to crystal singing, and Killashandra may have discovered a way to help all crystal singers. Because of her courage and open-mindedness, and her adept crystal singing, Killashandra receives a great gift from the alien, just as Helva had received the ability to be with Niall from the alien Corviki. Art provides communication and benefit to both alien and human. Crystal singing provides a way to enhance art over time, as Killashandra gloats: "Singing crystal was so much more rewarding than being a mere concert singer, who could expect only three of four decades of 'good' voice! She was still 'singing' after a hundred and ninety-seven years" (*Crystal Line* 295).

Art also provides a bridge between brain ships and crystal singers. In *Killashandra*, the CS 914, a brain ship named Samel and a brawn named Chadria, help Killashandra and others escape from Optheria. "[B]oth brain and brawn partners had been excellent hosts, with stories scurrilous and amusing" (352), and Samel and Chadria even team up to play tri-dimensional games with their passengers. In *Crystal Line*, the relationship between crystal singers and brain ships is developed even more. Piloted by a brain ship without a brawn because any "normal" human would be endangered by the alien crystal, Killashandra and her partner Lars develop fondness for Brendan, a brain ship. Killashandra thinks to herself "Of all the myriad manifestations of humans, altered or otherwise, she most respected shell people—to a point of reverence. . . . Traveling with Brendan was truly an honor" (18). Brendan repays the compliment by describing the crystal singers as "soft shells" (20). They work as a team, functioning as Brendan's brawns as they contact the alien on Opal. Brendan even sings, though not in as many voices or as well as the legendary Helva, who is said to still be alive. This sympathy between crystal singers and brain ships underscores the parallels between the two creations.

Theme of Sexuality

In one important area, however, crystal singers differ from brain ships in that they allow McCaffrey to explore human sexuality more explicitly. There is tremendous sensuality and physical stimulation in singing crystal. Throughout *The Crystal Singer* series, McCaffrey describes singing crystal as sensual, even dangerously so. The process of singing crystal turns out to be reciprocal, and the best crystal singers are those who pay attention to their "partners." As Killashandra explains it, "It isn't so much as singing crystal then, as being sung to be crystal" (*Crystal Singer* 169). The crystal she discovers is almost personified, and she responds to it as she does a human lover. She weeps with joy as the sun strikes black crystal making music that "seeped through her skin to intoxicate her senses" (*Crystal Singer* 215). Killashandra experiences singing crystal as "that pleasurable nerve-caressing distraction, as if a highly-skilled lover were inside her body" (*Crystal Singer* 218). The danger emerges when storms appear, and the sensual delights of singing crystal cause the singer to ignore the dangerous weather. Such intense physical pleasures are augmented when crystal singers sing duets. Because they carry crystal emanations in their bodies, liaisons with non-crystal singers are particularly overwhelming for "normal" humans, making crystal singers dangerous but attractive lovers.

While Killashandra finds physical pleasure in crystal singing, she also finds pleasure with human lovers. In her long life she enjoys many brief unions, and McCaffrey makes it clear that "morning song," the ecstatic union of two crystal singers after cutting crystal, can and is enjoyed in heterosexual and homosexual partners. In *Killashandra,* the crystal singer is even warned against breaking up the partnering of an all-female space ship. The two great loves of Killashandra's life, Lanzecki and Lars Dahl, are both accomplished crystal singers, and both head the Heptite Guild, with Lars succeeding Lanzecki. Her sexual experiences with both men are compared favorably with singing crystal. The implication is that being an accomplished artist means that you are also sexually accomplished. As she does with Moreta in *The Dragonriders of Pern* series, McCaffrey creates in Killashandra a healthy, lusty, and admirable role model. The symbiont's side effect of sterility means that Killashandra cannot bear children, a loss she does regret briefly when she first meets Lars. But instead of biological children, Killashandra and Lars take over the Heptite Guild and revitalize it. With her newly restored memory and her example of cooperation for the usually solitary and suspicious crystal singers, Killashandra teaches crystal singers to work together to gather more crystal. As Helva channels her mothering instincts to help humanity as a whole, so does Killashandra direct her energies to the Heptite Guild and the needs of beings throughout Federated Sentient Planets. The reader realizes, as Killashandra does, that her full partnership with Lars is more than sufficient for happiness; "more than friend, lover, partner, and alter ego" (*Crystal Line* 295). Like Helva, at the end of *The Crystal Singer* series Killashandra has found a mate who fulfills her completely. McCaffrey's inclusion of an active sexual life as part of both Killashandra's and Helva's needs shows that these two series are adult in their explicit acknowledgment of the importance of sexuality to human existence. Like art, sexuality enhances and enriches human existence. And like Helva and Killashandra, McCaffrey seems to ask her readers to believe that despite formidable obstacles (such as Helva's encased body or Killashandra's flawed memory), such love can and will be found.

ALTERNATE READING: MYTH CRITICISM

As discussed in Chapter 2, Ursula Le Guin has said, "Science fiction is the mythology of the modern world," and no novelist perhaps best exemplifies the truth of her statement than Anne McCaffrey, especially in her *Brain Ship* and *Crystal Singer* series. Reading these series in terms of myth enables us to see the truth in Le Guin's statement. Every culture has myths, stories that help people make sense of the world. Myths provide explanations and a sense of order. They explain the inexplicable—how the world began and why things are the way they are. Myths frequently contain origin stories, about how and why humanity was created. While we can clearly see that Greek myths are fantastical, our own myths seem appropriate. One of our most mythical narratives is the narrative of science. Many people believe that through science we can understand how our world was created, where human beings came from, and many other events including the weather, illness, and so on. Science fiction is one site of scientific myth that is explicitly fictional, but very much about why and how human culture exists. Science fiction draws on earlier mythical figures, such as that of the witch and siren, to blend old and new myths. Furthermore, reading contemporary science fiction in terms of myth allows us to see literature as a continuum, stretching from ancient stories up to our modern retellings.

Throughout *The Brain Ship* series, the brains are frequently referred to as being magical and witchlike. For instance, Helva is called "silver-plated sorceress" (*The Ship Who Sang* 43), "Cinderella" (*Get Off the Unicorn* 282), and "tin-plated witch" (*The Ship Who Sang* 227). Her use of seductive singing to beguile and finally kill her tormenting kidnapper evokes the myth of the sirens, who used their singing to lure men to their death at sea. Helva and the other female brain ships also provide a modern version of the personification of ships as female. Similarly, Killashandra's singing and the power of her crystal aura create fear and respect in those who encounter her. The description of a crystal singer as "a silicate spider, paralyzing its prey" (*Crystal Singer* 28), also evokes the siren enthralling her victim. Killashandra's remarkable lovemaking leaves a mark on those fortunate enough to love her. The Ballybran symbiont makes Killashandra virtually immortal, as does Helva's encasement in her ship. Their immortality is one of the features that makes these two characters mythical. They are larger-than-life, because their lifespans so exceed that of normal humans. As a result they have experiences and perspectives that are superhuman.

A legend has even been created about crystal singers that claims "that a crystal singer can sound notes that'll drive a man mad. That they lure men to them, seduce them, and then kidnap 'em away to Ballybran, and they never come back" (*Crystal Line* 177). The crystal singers are a positive, feminist version of sirens. This legend, as do all legends in McCaffrey's worlds, has a basis in fact. Because lovemaking and crystal singing are analogous activities, lovemaking helps crystal singers forget crystal when they are off Ballybran. Like other crystal singers, Killashandra has many such relationships, the first when she is not yet a singer and Carrik, a crystal singer, introduces her to sex and to crystal. Crystal singers recruit other singers in this fashion—if their lovers have perfect pitch. But they are required to be honest and forthright about the dangers of crystal singing, and recruits have their own reasons, like Killashandra's failed career, to become crystal singers. But the aura of seduction and romance lingers with the crystal singers. McCaffrey revises the myth of the siren to suggest that sexuality and seduction have a place in human society—that sex is natural, and pleasurable, and, perhaps most radically, women too have a right to assert and enjoy their sexual desires.

While there are structural similarities to evil female mythic creatures,

McCaffrey revises the figures of the witch and the siren so that they become positive figures. While some people she encounters fear Helva, the reader knows that Helva is innately benevolent, and every story depicts Helva rescuing humans and helping humanity by bringing it the advanced technology of the Corviki. Similarly, while Killashandra can be quite forbidding, and is quite willing to play the "high priestess routine" (*Crystal Singer* 293), she uses her powers benignly—to install crystal, to assist crucial communications, to rescue people from illegal subliminal conditioning. As she recasts these traditional figures of feminine evil, McCaffrey joins the ranks of other contemporary science fiction writers like Mercedes Lackey, Andre Norton, James Schmitz, Joan D. Vinge, Joan Slonczewski, and many others.

Science fiction writers are particularly well suited to remake myth because of the genre's qualities (see Chapter 2). Myth by its very nature must be fabulous, extraordinary, and larger-than-life. Extrapolation, or developing from what exists to what might be, logically, functions in McCaffrey's work with the figure of the witch. Through the science fiction setting of the future, McCaffrey can depict female characters with powers that are even more formidable than those of actual witches. Through the science fiction feature of the alien, McCaffrey can depict beings with powers that enable them to transform Helva so that she isn't mentally confined by her ship, and Killashandra so she is spared memory loss. Most importantly, perhaps, McCaffrey can use the appeal and popularity of science fiction to send her message of female empowerment to a mass audience.

6

The Rowan Series

In *The Rowan* (1990), *Damia* (1992), *Damia's Children* (1993), and *Lyon's Pride* (1994), McCaffrey creates a family saga spanning three generations. In the tradition of mainstream novelists like Anthony Trollope and Belva Plain, McCaffrey constructs a series of novels that follows a family over generations. This paradigm appears frequently in the mainstream novel, but as McCaffrey employs the family saga within a science fiction frame she combines two genres. The reader thus enjoys the trials and tribulations of a family, but also experiences the action and excitement of a science fiction space opera, a colorful action-adventure story set in space.

The four novels in *The Rowan* series also draw on concepts from an earlier book by McCaffrey, *To Ride Pegasus*, a linked collection of short stories. A sequel to this collection, *Pegasus in Flight* (1990), provides a bridge between *To Ride Pegasus* and *The Rowan* series. (*To Ride Pegasus* and *Pegasus in Flight* have been published together as *The Wings of Pegasus*). In *To Ride Pegasus* (1973), a traffic accident leads to the first scientific proof of mental powers when a clairvoyant named Henry Darrow suffers a head injury. To heal him, doctors apply the Goosegg, a device that measures brain patterns, to his injury. The results show electrical impulses as the clairvoyant sees the future, thus proving scientifically the existence of extrasensory perception, or psionic power. Being able to measure telepathy on a machine provides proof of its existence as a biological activity. Here McCaffrey cleverly skirts a classic division between science fiction and fantasy literature by having "magic" turn out to be "science" (see Chapter 2). Psionics, as mental powers are known in science fiction, encompass a wide range of skills; in McCaffrey's universe, most psychics have one particular ability, such as being able to see the future or to communicate mentally.

In *To Ride Pegasus* Henry Darrow founds a Parapsychic Center to protect other psychics known as Talents. While that book depicts the struggles of Talents to become socially and legally accepted, *The Rowan* series is set in a future in which Talents have become an integral part of an interstellar star network, valued for their ability to defend planets from alien invasion. *Pegasus in Flight* focuses on two young Talents: Tirla, a girl who lives in a slum, and Peter Reidinger, a boy who appears prominently in *The Rowan* series as an elder statesman for Talents. *Pegasus in Flight* depicts the early history of the man who, as Earth Prime, the leader of all psychics, carefully nurtures the young Rowan in *The Rowan*. *To Ride Pegasus*, then, should be read as a general precursor to *The Rowan* series, which builds on the ideas of psionic Talent into the future, where on a nine-planet system the Talents are widely admired and respected. *Pegasus in Flight* reveals how and why Talents assume such a prominent role in the galaxy. In *The Rowan* series the types and quality of Talent are clearly identified, and each Talent is ranked by number. The designation of T-1, or Prime, signifies psionic Talent of the highest ability and greatest variety; T-2 signifies less ability, and so on. A Prime Talent, like Rowan and many members of her family, is very rare and extremely powerful. Prime Talents staff Towers on planets and satellites that serve as transfer points for material throughout the nine-planet system. At these Towers, lesser Talents work with the Prime Talent, augmenting their powers by working together. While the Talents' positions are secure in *The Rowan* series, they still face prejudice because of their difference from other human beings, and, even more importantly, they must struggle to control and harness their Talent. Like Andre Norton, whose extremely popular *Witch World* series deals with similar issues, or James Schmitz, the author of *The Witches of Karres*, McCaffrey uses Talent or magic to create characters who make critical interventions in their worlds. Unlike Norton or Schmitz, however, McCaffrey writes for an adult audience and deals explicitly with sexuality.

SERIES DEVELOPMENT

In this series of connected novels, McCaffrey uses the conceit of Talent to explore a wide range of social and psychological issues from racism and other forms of prejudice, to feminism and the representation of art. In each book, McCaffrey focuses on the development of a character or a character and her or his family. The plots can be traced back to a pattern that appears first in McCaffrey's short fiction. Through the exploration of her character's development, McCaffrey uses Talent to explore what it means to be human. Her characters struggle to find love, acceptance, and an understanding of how to live with difference.

McCaffrey created Rowan's family in two short stories published in *Get Off the Unicorn* (1977): "Lady in the Tower" and "A Meeting of Minds." In an introduction, McCaffrey describes "Lady" as "the story I prefer to acknowledge as my first" (1). She describes the two stories as "unashamed love stories" and explains, "That's what I do best: combining either science fact or fantasy with heterogeneous inter-reaction" (1). "Lady" focuses on Rowan's discovery of her partner, Jeff Raven, and "Meeting" depicts Rowan's daughter, Damia, finding her true love. While these are engaging love stories, McCaffrey's development of the characters and expansion of the plots to full-length novels complicates the straightforward "love stories." McCaffrey identifies the key to *The Rowan* series when she describes Rowan and Damia as "good strong characters" (2). She explains that her interest in Talent developed into the collection *To Ride Pegasus*, and hints at *The Rowan* series' inevitability: "Who knows when I'll write about that third generation" (2). Fortunately for her readers, McCaffrey has found time, and she combines the Talent depicted in *To Ride Pegasus* with engaging strong characters to create the third generation of Rowan's family.

Talent works very differently from the Impressing of dragons in *The Dragonriders of Pern* series (see Chapter 4), the cybernetic interface with machine in *The Brain Ship* series (see Chapter 5), or the relationship of crystal singer to crystal in *The Crystal Singer* series (see Chapter 5). While dragonriders bond with their dragons, and brains depend on their ships for all sensory input, and crystal singers need to return to the planet Ballybran to cut crystal to survive, Talent requires no other being. While the Talents in these novels yearn for a partner, their Talents are individual and self-sustaining. The Talents merge minds to create a stronger psionic power, subsuming their identities in a group effect. Talents must also choose mates. In this regard, the Talents in *The Rowan* series are more like "normal" human beings than many of McCaffrey's other characters. Talent also involves less choice than the other extraordinary skills McCaffrey depicts in her other series. In *The Rowan* series a character is born with a particular Talent, and while circumstances may help the Talent emerge, Talent cannot be taught or induced. Because of these qualities, McCaffrey's Talents have to rely more on themselves and on family members than do crystal singers, dragonriders, or brain ships. Like these three groups, however, Talents are separated, admired, and sometimes feared by other human beings. Depicting special individuals allows McCaffrey to examine the weaknesses and strengths of human societies as she examines how well (or badly) humans cope with difference.

PLOT DEVELOPMENT

The Rowan

The Rowan establishes the parameters of the series: the extraordinary psionic powers that Rowan enjoys, as well as her resultant struggle to find identity and a place for herself; the themes of tolerance and psychological development; and feminist issues of the female alien and the mind versus the machine. Rowan, the heroine of the first book, discovers her Talent, her psionic or mental abilities, when she is a toddler, the only survivor of a mining camp swallowed up by a mud slide. Trapped in an air pocket, the child broadcasts a planet-wide cry for help, demonstrating her extraordinary telepathic powers. When she is slightly older, she demonstrates equally unusual telekinetic power, the ability to transport herself and other objects through space. In *The Rowan*, we follow the orphaned child as she discovers her identity and purpose. Because of her tremendous abilities, the child becomes known as "The Rowan," an appellation that reflects her tremendous powers and solitary position in its inhumanity as she has the name of a camp rather than a family. "The Rowan" eventually becomes plain "Rowan" to her friends and adopted family. Rowan founds a dynasty of extraordinary Talents, and it is their adventures that are charted in the other three novels. Even in these subsequent books, Rowan remains a powerful presence and her actions provide a turning point for the plot. While the primary focus in the later books may be younger protagonists, McCaffrey makes sure we keep in mind the power of the matriarch by giving Rowan important roles to play, as for example, in *Lyon's Pride*, when Rowan merges mentally with one of her grandsons to teleport themselves and move an enormous alien ship. Each novel in the series follows the plot development of the first: We watch an extraordinarily gifted individual struggle with the strengths and weaknesses of his or her Talent.

In *The Rowan*, the plot follows the main character through a series of crises and developments. The crises begin when Rowan's life is endangered during a mudslide, continue when she is attacked as an adolescent by a gang of thugs, and move to a huge scale when an alien species threatens the entire human race. In each case, Rowan defeats her opponents, and as she does, she develops. The reader sees Rowan change gradually from a toddler to a mature, sexually active woman. Throughout the novel, we identify and sympathize with Rowan because she is a likeable outsider.

Damia

Damia covers part of the same time period that is covered in *The Rowan*, but instead of focusing on Rowan, we see events through the eyes of Afra Lyon, who works with Rowan as a number two Talent in her tower, and from the perspective of Rowan's daughter, Damia. This bifurcation of the single protagonist in *The Rowan* develops through the series; the last two novels focus on a number of Rowan's grandchildren. The shift emphasizes the themes rather than character development so important in *The Rowan*. As in *The Rowan*, *Damia* begins with a child, but the child is Afra, rather than Damia. McCaffrey utilizes this overlap to emphasize how the interpretation of events is subjective, depending on the perspective of the narrator. The novel continues through the events covered in *The Rowan*, and beyond. Damia is Rowan's third child, and Jeff, Rowan's husband and Damia's father, describes her as "very much like her mother" (*Damia* 147) in temperament and in her extraordinary psionic abilities. Like Rowan, Damia finds that her abilities separate her from others.

Like her mother, Damia is a powerful Talent and a likeable, though obstreperous personality. As a third child, Damia is often left out or left behind; she must find her own path and mature into an adult. Like Rowan, Damia often faces danger, including dangerous aliens. The plot moves according to these crises in Damia's life. At the end of the novel,

Damia has discovered love with Afra, and she is expecting their first child.

Damia's Children

The novel opens with the aliens, called Mrdinis or 'Dinis for short, hunting the family's supper with Laria, one of Damia's children. In contrast to the other books in the series, *Damia's Children* focuses on four of Damia's offspring, instead of the eponymous heroines of the first two books. As a result, this novel emphasizes thematic issues more than character development. McCaffrey provides much less psychological detail, and most of the plot revolves around the description of the two alien species, the 'Dinis, friends to the humans, and the Hivers. Each of Damia's children confronts dilemmas connected to working with their Talent and dealing with aliens. As in the first two novels, this book emphasizes the importance of accepting difference. Damia's children demonstrate even more awareness and openness to the viewpoints of others because these children have been raised with aliens from birth. Damia and Afra's willingness to raise their children with alien young reveals that they have internalized the lessons of tolerance so important to Talents.

Lyon's Pride

The most recent addition to *The Rowan* series by no means resolves the family saga, or the problem of how to coexist with very different species. But while the series' drama remains unresolved, *Lyon's Pride* does reveal significant development in some of the series' themes. A prologue to *Lyon's Pride* covers the events of the first three novels. The Lyon of the title refers to Damia's children, here identified by their father's surname, Lyon. Action revolves around Laria, Rojer, and Thian, Damia's children, who bring pride to the Lyon family through their careful and judicious use of their Talent. Using their Talent, the children—now young adults—continue to bridge gaps between alien species. Laria becomes the first Prime on Clarf, the Mrdini homeworld. Sharing human psionic Talent with the Mrdini provides one means of establishing trust in the relationship. With his childhood Mrdini friends, Laria's brother Rojer works aboard a spaceship tracing the Hiver civilization. While not precisely analogous to a dragonrider's bond with his or her dragon, Rojer does share a special and unique intimacy with his Mrdini friends. Consequently, Rojer faces incredible sorrow when he watches as his friends, Kat and Gil, are murdered by another Mrdini who orders them to direct missiles against the Hivers. Like Rojer, Kat and Gil agree that the Hivers should not wantonly or callously be destroyed, and the Mrdinis give up their lives so that the Hivers and Rojer can live. Rojer's love for his murdered friends and their unselfishness are rewarded when they are restored to life through a reengineering of their bodies, and humans learn more about Mrdini reproduction and values. While his siblings live and work with Mrdinis, Thian works with his grandmother Rowan, and Flavia, another Prime. Together they merge to push ships out in a further search for Hiver ships. Thian eventually finds a suitable mate, a union that signals hope for the future.

CHARACTER DEVELOPMENT

The Female Heroine

The Rowan exemplifies McCaffrey's interest in the creation and development of a young woman with extraordinary powers. While Rowan has some mentors, her emotional and psychic development really rests with her alone. We meet Rowan just as she has been abruptly and cruelly orphaned by a disaster that kills not only her parents and brother, but also an entire community. But, as she will throughout the series, and as her daughter and grandchildren will, Rowan takes responsibility for herself. Drawing on and developing her psychic ability to communicate over immense distance, Rowan broadcasts a cry for help that disrupts the entire planet. She is rescued not just because she deserves to be, but because she makes her plight known and refuses to give up. This determination and will to survive see Rowan through several crises. After this first tragic loss of her family, Rowan experiences other traumatic losses—that of her beloved empathic doll, and her foster mother. Each loss makes her stronger. From her pain, Rowan forges new strength and identity. But she doesn't make the mistake that her teacher, Siglen, makes—she doesn't isolate herself completely. Rowan needs and draws upon others—her foster mother, her first lover, and then eventually, her true love and equal, Jeff. In Rowan, McCaffrey creates a female heroine who is strong and independent, but who also manifests the traditionally feminine values of love and nurturance. As a result of her balance of independence and cooperation, Rowan saves lives and is rewarded with a dynasty of her own Talented and loveable family.

Damia similarly provides a psychological novel of development for Rowan's daughter and for Afra, Rowan's friend who becomes Damia's husband. While Damia is not orphaned as Rowan is, Damia endures a difficult childhood, because she is alienated from her older brother and sister who have a close psychological bond. Feeling like an outsider in her own family, Damia relishes the company of Coonie, a raccoonlike creature, and Rascal, her mother's barquecat (a rare space cat), who seem drawn to her. With their help, at the tender age of two, Damia uses her Talent to get into life-threatening scrapes when she wanders around the space station by herself; once she is almost killed and is only saved by Afra's teleportation abilities. When Rowan develops a pregnancy-related illness, Damia and her brother and sister are packed off to Deneb to live with their grandmother. There Damia grows and matures through several emotional crises.

The Couple

Decades apart in age, Afra and Damia each face a difficult maturation as they confront their differences. Afra is raised on a strict "methody" (4), or religious society that frowns on drinking and smoking and "hanky panky" (4) on the planet Capella. From his infancy, Afra is wild and unwilling to conform, as Damia will be twenty years later. Afra seeks out and befriends a space captain, who explains racial difference to the young Afra when Afra is called "a pint-sized greenie" (4). Afra also learns the ancient ethnic art form origami from the space captain. Through this relationship with an outsider, Afra demonstrates his maturity and acceptance of difference. Damia too confronts prejudice when she encounters it at a school on Deneb, where she and her siblings have been sent to live with their grandmother while their mother is ill. At school, "Damia quickly learned the fallacy of judging a person on the color of skin, condition of body, or the attractiveness of face" (181). While such prejudice is considered "intolerable" (181) in the Talented, other humans still cling to prejudice. Damia faces it at school when an un-Talented boy throws a rock at Damia's Talented brother, Larak, during a dodgeball game. When Damia prevents the rock from hitting Larak the rock strikes her in the head. Afra intervenes to keep the unTalented boy, Teval, from being expelled, and Teval is assigned to teach Damia self-defense. She also learns to forgive and understand the source of Teval's pain—he had lost his entire family in the Beetle attack on Deneb. This picture of amity provides an example of McCaffrey's response to prejudice of all kinds. It can be conquered only by understanding, and developing this type of understanding is essential to maturing as an adult.

Damia must also learn to forgive herself as she is involved in situations that cause harm to others. As a wild young adolescent, Damia has sex with a T-9, a Talent ranking much lower than hers, and her greater Talent "burns out" the less powerful man's psionic capabilities. For years, Damia becomes involved only with unTalented lovers, unable to risk such a tragedy again. Then Damia, Afra, and Larek (Damia's beloved brother) fight off a malign alien force, but Larek dies in the struggle and Afra and Damia are seriously injured. Isolated to heal, Afra teaches Damia to forgive herself, and to take the risk of loving him. As Damia overlooks their age and Talent differences, she is rewarded with peace and contentment that has previously eluded her. Damia learns to accept and control her Talent, signalling her maturity.

GENRE

In *The Rowan* series, McCaffrey deals with social issues: the maturation of the individual, including the growth and development of the artist; the position of the outsider and the importance of tolerance and the acceptance of difference. *The Rowan* can be read as examples of bildungsroman, novels that depict psychological development of an individual and kunstlerroman, a fiction that represents the growth and development of an artist. Both these literary forms are important not only to these particular novels but also to the series as a whole (as well as McCaffrey's other books), because elements of the bildungsroman and kunstlerroman shape all her texts. Exploring McCaffrey's use of these literary forms helps us understand her interest in and use of psychology and art. McCaffrey's fictions reveal a deep and continuing interest in human character and in how art can be used to explore facets of human psychology. Her characters and plots suggest that art (represented by singing, acting, or in *The Rowan* series, Talent) has a pivotal position in maintaining and protecting humanity.

Bildungsroman

As *The Rowan* charts Rowan's growth and development and search for identity, it follows the classic pattern of the bildungsroman, the novel type that follows a protagonist from childhood to adulthood. Charles Dickens' *Great Expectations* and Charlotte Brontë's *Jane Eyre* are famous nineteenth-century examples of bildungsroman in the traditional novel. This novel of psychological development explores the needs and desires of a growing child. In many bildungsroman, the author encourages the reader to identify and sympathize with the struggles of an outsider by narrating the novel's events from the protagonist's perspective. Like Pip from *Great Expectations* and Jane from *Jane Eyre*, Rowan is orphaned and uncertain of her identity. Rowan is named after the mining camp where she was found because no one knows for certain who her parents were. Her unusual name signifies her separation from all others on her planet; Rowan is separated from others because of her tremendous Talent, her silver hair, and her unusual rearing. From the very beginning, Rowan is depicted as a likeable and engaging child, dealing with a tragic situation and unusual powers. Like Jane Eyre, however, Rowan wrestles with a sense of injustice and mistreatment. Given a pukha, "a specially programmed stabilizing surrogate device," (29) as Rowan herself describes it, Rowan uses it as her alter ego, confiding and talking to it much as Jane Eyre talks to "Reason" and "Fancy," as though they were real people. Isolated from other people, Rowan grows up relying on her own instincts. Her guardian, Lusena, has Talent, but to a much lesser degree than Rowan. When Lusena, her two nieces, and Rowan go on vacation, the older niece Moira, spitefully jealous of Rowan, destroys her pukha, and Rowan must learn not to strike out with her powers. Rowan must also learn to get by without her pukha. Its loss represents a major turning point for the now adolescent protagonist. She is presented with the rare and adorable barquecat, Rascal, but it remains a pet and does not serve the same function as her pukha doll. Rowan must internalize her alter ego as a part of the maturation process. The novel also depicts Rowan's sexual maturation, as she chooses her first lover and then eventually a permanent mate. By the end of the novel, Rowan's adult status is marked by her pregnancy and by her dramatic rescue of the human race from an alien threat. Both experiences signal her acceptance of adult responsibilities.

McCaffrey combines the features of a bildungsroman with those of science fiction. The tropes of science fiction, such as psionic Talent, armed conflict, and aliens, rely on defamiliarization, the process of taking what is familiar (psychological development) and placing it in another context. Through this defamiliarization readers can enjoy and learn from the literary form of the *bildungsroman*.

Kunstlerroman

Dealing with Rowan's Talent makes *The Rowan* analogous to a kunstlerroman, a novel that charts the development of an artist. James Joyce's *Portrait of an Artist as a Young Man* exemplifies this novelistic tradition. In Joyce's novel, he portrays a young child whose perceptions are sharper than other people's, showing that he is inherently artistic. The protagonist must come to terms with his difference from other people and learn how to create art. Similarly, Rowan's Talent causes her to see and perceive the world differently. The novel depicts her struggle to find a place for herself. She does so literally when she transforms the apartment given to her by her teacher Siglen, the only other Prime Talent on their planet Altair, into a place of beauty and repose, using her telekinetic powers to move objects and to paint the rooms. In a more general way, however, Rowan's Talent is itself an art. She must be trained by Siglen, but she must also train herself to use telekinesis and telepathy to help others. Rowan bravely overcomes agoraphobia (fear of open spaces), accidentally implanted in her psyche by Siglen, to come to the rescue of another Talent on a colony planet; she also uses her abilities to heal through touch. As in any kunstlerroman, *The Rowan* shows the difficulties and necessities for the artist of learning how to use his or her art. Like *The Ship Who Sang* or *The Crystal Singer*, *The Rowan* explores what it means to be a gifted individual and to be set apart from the rest of humanity. At the same time, *The Rowan* stresses what other kunstlerromans do, the importance of art to society. Rowan's Talent literally saves the human race, emphasizing that the care and finances devoted to her education were well worth the expenditure. As a singer and writer herself (see Chapter 1), McCaffrey uses the patterns of science fiction to remind her readers how much art has to offer human beings.

THEMES

The Rowan series reveals the development of major themes that appear in lesser or greater degree in other McCaffrey novels. The depiction of the outsider, the use of the female alien, the conflict between mind and machine, the importance of community, and the necessity of tolerance connect the novels in this series. The themes all relate to McCaffrey's overarching concerns about gender and relationships. In this series, as in her other careful and engaging depictions of worlds and characters, McCaffrey involves her reader in issues that raise ethical and social concerns about the treatment of individuals in a social context.

The Outsider

Part of being Talented means dealing with being an outsider. As a Prime Talent, Rowan is separated not only from the unTalented, but also from most other Talents. As an orphan, Rowan is further alienated from the tight family structure of Altair, the planet to which her parents migrated to work in the mining camp destroyed by the mudslide. She has no parents, brothers, or sisters, and until the end of the novel she does not know her family name. When Earth Prime, the Talent in charge of all others, assembles a training group on Altair, Rowan must pretend to be only a T-4 so that the other young students will accept her. She similarly deceives the young captain she chooses to be her lover because she feels he will reject her if he knows the full extent of her powers. While her experience in the training group is satisfying, Rowan longs for the company of an equal. She is promoted to running her own Tower of Talents, moving material and personnel through Callisto, an installation on one of Jupiter's moons, to other points and other planets. But as the Head of a Tower she is very lonely. Like Killashandra from *Crystal Singer*, Rowan has the temper of a high-strung performer, and her co-workers fear and respect her. McCaffrey seems to justify or at least explain Rowan's occasionally outrageous prima donna behavior by suggesting that she *is* a prima donna of the Talent, and that the strain of leading a Tower without companionship is wearing. While the narrator informs us that some of Rowan's co-workers threaten to quit, we also see that they are easily bribed back with a few favors and an apology from Rowan. Though she tries their patience, they are fond of her.

McCaffrey sympathetically depicts the struggles of a gifted individual who, because of her gifts and upbringing, remains outside of society, even the society of the Talented.

Coping with being an outsider also shapes *Pegasus in Flight*, as the three main characters (Rhyssa, Tirla, and Peter) also struggle with being outsiders. Rhyssa fights for all Talents as their leader and negotiator. She must confront prejudice against Talents, as well as a desire to ruthlessly exploit them. She and another Talent, Dorotea, ''were always subtly mentioning [to Peter] how important it was not to rub Talent into people's noses. People resented differences. Talent had always to be discreet'' (179). As an undocumented child, Tirla is outside all government benefits and she must struggle to eke out an existence. In addition, like other undocumented children, she is in danger of being abducted and being sold as a slave. Peter's upbringing has been more conventional, but he must deal with rejection from his family and others when he is paralyzed. As he learns to use his extraordinary Talent to replace muscular control, and eventually to launch ships, Peter must adapt to his outsider status caused by his youth and superlative skills. It is his paralysis that creates the impetus for his powers to emerge, and other crises threatening the lives of many humans that cause him to stretch his power to their fullest.

Similarly, it takes the appearance of a crisis and a truly alien outsider to bring Rowan to the height of her powers. The crisis also produces an equal for her to love—an untrained Talent from the colony planet of Deneb. Through this plot twist, McCaffrey suggests that even so alienated an outsider as Rowan can find an appropriate partner. Because readers identify with Rowan, McCaffrey reassures her readers, who may also feel alienated, that someday they too will find someone to care for who will care for them. This reassurance may be especially relevant for McCaffrey's adolescent readers, who will find a parallel in Rowan's experiences in their own adjustment to society and the roles required of them.

The theme of the outsider also appears in *Lyon's Pride*, but with some significant permutations, as the message of acceptance becomes extended to the Hivers and to homosexuals. McCaffrey's undramatic inclusion of important homosexual characters in this novel reminds readers that there are prejudices on Earth that are as unreasonable and painful as the conflicts she depicts between alien species. McCaffrey makes explicit what has been implicit in her philosophy all along—the application of tolerance to real-life situations on Earth.

The Female Alien

The climax of *The Rowan* occurs when the human race is threatened by an alien invasion. Rowan first learns of the danger when she is suddenly contacted by a Talent she doesn't know. This mind, which she first refers to as "Deneb" (his planet of origin), is part of a warm, loving, and extremely Talented untrained family, the Ravens. Even though Jeff Raven, the mental voice she knows as "Deneb," is the most Talented on his planet, he cannot fight off the alien invasion by himself, and he turns to Rowan for help. The aliens who are attacking Deneb are ruthlessly single-minded and well-equipped to take over a human planet. Using virus after virus, the aliens attempt to eradicate all life on Deneb, which they plan to colonize.

The aliens appear to be a version of a beetle, with hard wings and multiple legs with digits. There is one large specimen, the queen, and numerous eggs. The alien is that most dangerous of aliens in science fiction—the female alien. As discussed in Chapter 2, the female alien presents the most danger to humans because through the power of reproduction, the female alien has the capability to overwhelm mankind. In Mary Shelley's *Frankenstein* and Orson Scott Card's *Ender's Game* the female alien is depicted unsympathetically, but McCaffrey presents a more complex characterization of the female alien. Her female aliens, the "beetles," are powerful and dangerous, and they escape the destruction that is the fate of Shelley's female creature and Card's buggers. Instead, the "beetles" remain a viable threat, and their captured queen evokes sympathy, especially from certain Talents. McCaffrey suggests that even your enemies should be treated well and carefully.

Card resuscitates his buggers and their race is rejuvenated after massive human remorse for the extermination masterminded by a young human boy, but creating sympathy for a completely destroyed enemy is quite different from devising a complex portrait of a viable competitor. McCaffrey, like other feminist science fiction writers, uses the female alien to stress the power of the feminine, where Card and other male writers use the female alien to glorify the power of the masculine. Card's female aliens are destroyed and revived by a young boy whom the military has trained to be a killer. McCaffrey, on the other hand, uses female Talents to locate and control the threat that the "beetles" represent.

While Card depicts a male destroying a female race, McCaffrey shows human females understanding a female alien.

While Rowan's mind merges with all the other Talents on her Tower to defeat the two alien ships, Deneb is again threatened by invasion at the very end of the novel. This time, however, the humans have some warning, because of the special intuitive powers of Rowan, her mother-in-law Isthia, and other female Talents. They all sense anger and pain, which they determine isn't human but instead emanates from an alien ship. The anger and pain have been sublimated into determination, which the female Talents discover resides not in one mind but in a multiple mind—a hive mind. As Isthia explains, the "it" is " 'a many,' a feminine 'many' " (307). As Rowan understands it, "The female of the species has always been more deadly than the male" (310), and the former Earth Prime, concurs, analyzing the situation thus: " 'Defending its young. I suppose even beetles can have maternal imperatives' " (310). The female Talents are best suited to fight this menace; even Jeff, the strongest male Prime Talent, cannot hear the aura of the female aliens. Maternal instinct vies with maternal instinct, for Rowan now is a mother, and with her mother-in-law and other female Talents, strives to defeat the "beetles." They even arrange for female crews on the scout ships. What they soon discover is a planetoid bearing down on Deneb, a "mother ship" and "only females sense its intent" (314). The female Talents merge their minds, with Rowan as the leader, to destroy "the minds of the huge, female reproducers" (325) long enough for a merging of the male Talents to direct the planetoid into the sun. The other Talents praise Rowan as "the focus that saved us all" (328). Without Rowan's superior capability to direct their minds, all the Talents, and eventually all humans, would have been exterminated by the "beetles." Through this conflict between female Talent and a formidable female alien, McCaffrey suggests the power and strength of reproduction and of the feminine. In this regard, *The Rowan* repeats the feminist emphasis of McCaffrey's other series.

In *Damia's Children*, a name change for the aliens from Beetle to Hiver signals a shift away from seeing the aliens as the embodiment of their physical form—insects to be destroyed. The appellation Hiver depicts difference rather than disgust for their life form; Hiver describes their collective behavior and reproductive cycle. Both species display qualities that cause the humans to reflect on their own customs and beliefs. For example, the Hivers operate as a group mind, while humans merge minds only temporarily. The Hivers' lack of individualism appears a weakness that points to the strengths of human adaptability—the ability to work together and as individuals. McCaffrey depicts aliens very like Orson Scott Card's buggers in *Ender's Game*, who similarly pose a threat to human existence and who model insect life with a female queen. But where Card's young male hero succeeds in exterminating (for a while) the buggers, McCaffrey's Hivers remain alive and a source of contention for the human characters.

Because *Damia's Children* follows the lives of Damia's two daughters and two sons, the novel provides several instances that focus on gender differences in regard to the alien queen Hiver, who has been captured and imprisoned through Talent. Much is made of her femininity and her absolute control over the other members of her species. Damia's husband Afra sees her as a "praying mantis" (251) and one of Damia's daughters compares the queen to insects on Earth, some of whom eat the male after mating (268). At the same time, the alien queen's keeper more sympathetically describes her as "Like an actress waiting for her cue" (251). The careful reader of McCaffrey's novels realizes that this description is a sympathetic one, for many of her heroines are similarly described: Helva from *The Ship Who Sang* and Killashandra from *The Crystal Singer* (see Chapter 5).

Damia's children Zara and Rojer both feel "sadness and the queen's loneliness" (256), emotions that eventually galvanize Zara to visit the queen in her imprisonment. Gender differences play an important part in this action, too. Zara thinks that the queen's male keeper "was doing as well as a male could be expected to do. But the Hive queen was female. It had been females like her great-grandmother Isthia, and her great-aunts, Besseva and Rakella, who 'heard' the Hive response" (306). Zara's instinctive emphatic response seems conditioned in part by her menses, which have just begun. Her family fears that Zara will be a dysfunctional Talent, but with her empathic identification with the queen, Zara demonstrates great Talent as she teleports herself into the queen's chamber and discovers that the queen is dying from the cold. Zara's actions rescue the queen and demonstrate the importance of empathizing and identifying with others. While the Talents' actions in destroying the Hive ship that attacks them *are* defensible, mistreating the imprisoned queen is *not*. Zara's actions make clear the difference between self-defense and gratuitous violence. McCaffrey's novel suggests that empathy is more likely to be found in women, and that women's empathy should be heeded.

This message also shapes *Pegasus in Flight*, in which Peter's teacher comments negatively on the effect of masculine gender roles. *"All that manly repression has also been blocking Talent,"* (79) she realizes. In this regard McCaffrey's feminism follows a nineteenth-century feminist edict of separate spheres that valorized feminine sensitivity and nurturance. This notion of women's more nurturing sense of self and other was popularized in the twentieth century by Carol Gilligan's *In a Different Voice*. McCaffrey's Talents and alien queen can be read as a science fiction embodiment of Gilligan's view of feminine difference. While *Damia's Children* does not focus exclusively on a female protagonist, as the previous novels in this series do, McCaffrey's emphasis on and admiration for qualities identified as "feminine" continue in the sympathetic portrayal of the alien queen.

Other Aliens

The other aliens in *Damia's Children*, the Mrdini, also serve as a more benign contrast to human society. For example, the Mrdini use suicide as a military tactic—a tactic depicted as wasteful and destructive. The humans, especially the Talents, show the Mrdini another way to fight their common enemy, the Hivers. Because the Hivers ruthlessly colonize other planets, killing all life on them, both Mrdini and humans hate and fear the Hivers. While the Hivers have only a collective consciousness, humans and Mrdini are individuals and they value their independence and autonomy. In *Damia's Children* especially, McCaffrey draws on the characteristics of science fiction to examine human society. By depicting aliens and humans living together, McCaffrey allows her characters to explore human society from an outsider's perspective. As the human characters explain their society to the aliens and contrast it with alien customs, the reader begins to realize that human social customs are just that, customs, not innate or unalterable behavior. In this regard, McCaffrey's science fiction works in the same way that Michael Crichton's *Jurassic Park* or Arthur C. Clarke's *Rendezvous with Rama* does. Science fiction's depiction of disasters and aliens can teach humans to be cautious and careful with technology, and self-aware and critical of human social structures.

Mind vs. Machine

McCaffrey's feminist valorization of the "feminine" also appears in her emphasis on mental powers. In all of her fiction, psionics or mental abilities rival the power of machines. As discussed in Chapter 2, psionics has been associated with the feminine because psionics is frequently represented as magic. Machines, on the other hand, tend to be categorized as masculine because men have created and mastered machines. This polarization appears in *The Crystal Singer* series as well as in *The Rowan* series. While machines are important to the nine planet system, it is the Talents' psionic powers that enable communications and movement among the planets and beyond. A machine, the Goosegg, verified the existence of these powers, and machines such as spaceships are powered by a "mind-machine gestalt" using "telekinesis" (*The Rowan* 2). This breakthrough was "necessary to every aspect of the surge forward from the crowded and resources poor Earth" (2). In the Prologue to *The Rowan*, McCaffrey emphasizes the rarity of Talent, and its antecedent "probity," "neutrality," and "incorruptibil[ity]." This introduction encourages the reader to trust Rowan and other Talents. The history of Talents suggests they can and should be trusted implicitly.

The defeat of the aliens is entirely due to the Talents' mental abilities to turn away the virus-bearing missiles of the aliens and to sense and destroy the giant alien mother ship. In the first attack the armed Fleet of the Nine Star League, the government association of planets, could not possibly have arrived at Deneb in time to divert the invasion, and in the second the Fleet's powers are dwarfed by the second invasion's immense planetoid. Rowan characterizes the Armed Services thus: "The Armed Services, naval and military, regarded Talent with deep suspicion—since generally speaking, those of a mind to make war were too prosaic to understand minds which eschewed physical violence. Except of course, she reminded herself, when they needed an entire squadron dispatched to a far corner of the Galaxy. THEN they remembered Talent quite well!" (176–177). Rowan's description aptly captures the importance of Talents to the Armed Services, especially in the conflict with the immensely powerful aliens. Unaided by Talents, the machines of the Armed Services are inadequate. Similarly, the first contact with another new alien species occurs when Rowan's daughter Damia picks up an aura that mechanical devices have failed to detect (*Damia* 223). McCaffrey asserts that the most powerful technology that humans have is the one now least developed—

the powers of the mind. The connection of a Talent's powers to magic is repeated by Afra, when he calls Damia "witch" (*Damia* 201). Similarly, in *Pegasus in Flight*, Peter's teacher thinks that the mechanical devices that were supposed to correct Peter's paralysis inhibited his mental powers (79). In the same novel, Tirla's husband-to-be describes her as "The little witch" (246), and Tirla herself sees another Talent tracking her as "witchcraft" (171). By valorizing mental powers associated especially with women, McCaffrey suggests that we should look not to machines for salvation, but into our selves, especially that part of our humanity devalued as "feminine."

The Importance of Community

Throughout the series, McCaffrey repeats her themes of the importance of community and acceptance of difference. In *Damia*, an attitude of tolerance and understanding becomes crucial to the human race, as Damia and Afra encounter two new alien species—not the dreaded Hivers, but two races who contact Damia and Afra through a form of telepathy. McCaffrey implies that it is because of their early experience with prejudice that Afra and Damia are able to overcome the fear of the other and communicate with the aliens. Reinforcing the special powers of female Talents, Damia first contacts the alien mind Sodan, who proves to be a danger. Sodan is the last member of a race who travels through space without a body. Through this character, McCaffrey reveals the centrality of the body and bodily experiences even to humans who are Talented. Damia falls in love with Sodan out of loneliness. But Sodan cannot offer her physical love, and he plans to drain Damia of her extraordinary energy. Only by merging with Afra and her brother Larak can Damia resist Sodan's blandishments, and destroy him as he tries to kill her. Tragically, Larak dies in the fight.

Both the merging and Sodan's evil nature reveal McCaffrey's emphasis on community and relationships. Sodan's evil lies in part in his complete and total isolation as a sole surviving member of a species, and in his distaste for community: When he realizes that he cannot control Damia, he tries to destroy her community—Larak and Afra. After their tragic loss of Larak, Afra and Damia fall in love despite a 24-year age gap. As they recover in isolation, they receive odd dreams, which turn out to be communication from another alien species, the Mrdinis. Unlike the Hivers and Sodan, however, the Mrdinis are friendly and they request admission to the human system; they also fear and fight the Hivers. By opening to this contact, humans have found a powerful ally. The novel concludes with Damia's discovery of and joy in her pregnancy, a signal of a new beginning both for her, and, as it turns out, for the human race. McCaffrey thus endorses the importance of openness to communication from those who are radically different, even literally alien, and suggests how much communication has to offer.

As do the first two books in the series, *Damia's Children* stresses the importance of cooperation and the acceptance of difference. Three of Damia's children, Laria, Thian, and Rojer all work closely with a Mrdini pair, and a fourth child, Zara, empathizes with the alien queen Hiver and saves her from certain death. These four children encounter prejudice as they work with aliens: Laria confronts the prejudice of the other human ambassadors to the Mrdini homeworld; Thian deals with human prejudice and rigidity when he breaks protocol to save the life of one of his Mrdini friends who falls ill, and he is nearly murdered when he stops an effort to destroy Hiver larvae; Rojer feels sorrow at the isolation of the Hiver queen; Zara resists human prejudice against the Hiver queen when she uses her Talent to visit the queen in her isolation chamber on the lunar Heinlein Installation (a tribute to the famous science fiction writer, Robert Heinlein). The use of Heinlein's name functions both as a reference and as a revision. Heinlein is well known for his description of psionic powers in *Stranger in a Strange Land*, so that the installation's naming reflects McCaffrey's debt to Heinlein. At the same time, Heinlein's fictions are resolutely male-dominated and focused on father figures. McCaffrey's alien queen and matriarchal family of Talents provide a new view of Heinlein's patriarchal family. Of Heinlein, McCaffrey writes that he was one of the few major figures whom she didn't meet while she was an officer of the Science Fiction Writers of America. "I didn't LIKE the way Heinlein portrayed women . . . they certainly weren't variations that *I* as a woman, would recognize as female" (E-mail 3-14-95). In *The Rowan* series, McCaffrey has done a superb job of correcting Heinlein's omissions.

McCaffrey further revises Heinlein's justification of violence by showing in her novels that violence and hostility stem from an irrational dislike and fear of the other, the unknown. The queen has harmed no one. Because she was teleported to a secure station and has no other members of her species with her, she poses no threat to humanity. McCaffrey makes clear the instability and capriciousness of such feelings when she describes Thian's unknown assailant as "Malice," personifying the word. "Malice" fears Talents and the Hivers and wants only to hurt and destroy them. Although "Malice" proves quite powerful, with the help of his Talented family and other crew members, Thian survives—and so do the Hiver larvae, which are then sent to the queen. In other instances, Laria cannot change the prejudice of the official human envoys to the Mrdini world, but her understanding of Mrdini customs reassures the aliens and provides an antidote to the bureaucratic hostility. And finally, Zara's courageous intervention with the Hiver queen saves the queen's life. By the end of *Damia's Children*, humans and Mrdinis observe Hivers fighting and destroying each other—another signal lesson about the importance of cooperation and trust.

Tolerance

In *Lyon's Pride*, McCaffrey further develops the importance of the acceptance of difference, specifically in the context of the military. Through the character of Kincaid, McCaffrey depicts the pain caused by prejudice against homosexuals. Kincaid has been on a lengthy mission of space exploration, searching for Hivers. When he returns, he becomes Laria's number two in the Prime Tower on Clarf. Significantly, he replaces a Talent named Clarissia, who has made herself unbearable and obnoxious because of her irrational dislike for Mrdinis. She hates Mrdinis and Rowan's family; and as she leaves Clarf, Clarissia threatens them all. Her intolerance contrasts strikingly with Kincaid's easy acceptance of the aliens and life in the Tower. The Navy has strained Kincaid to the breaking point because of its intolerance and because of an emotional struggle he endured between two men. McCaffrey's depiction of an admirable and dedicated Talent who also happens to be homosexual brings her message of tolerance and acceptance to an important American social issue—the acceptance of homosexuals and lesbians in the U.S. military. In the context of the acceptance of alien life forms, the human Kincaid's sexual orientation makes very little difference at all. McCaffrey uses the aliens to suggest that as humans, no matter what our sexual orientation we belong and must learn to live and work together. This character provides a clear example of defamiliarization, which is discussed in Chapter 2 as one of the fundamental qualities of science fiction. By juxtaposing Kincaid's generous humanity with the inhumanity of alien species, McCaffrey shows how little difference sexual orientation makes—and how like other prejudices homophobia is.

The attitude of tolerance that McCaffrey advocates eventually extends also to the Hivers. Both humans and Mrdinis finally agree that the Hivers should not be exterminated, but that their joint mission will focus on preventing the Hive spheres from destroying other life forms. When they realize that the Hivers are "great farmers" (216), Zara and others contemplate a future in which the Hivers' "ability could be directed into proper channels" and "No one else would ever have to crop-farm" (216). This rosy vision of a future collaboration does not materialize in *Lyon's Pride*, but that the next generation can even conceive such amity provides promise. The main obstacle to cooperation is the human and Mrdini inability to communicate with the Hivers, but Zara's empathy for the queen suggests one possibility, and the discovery that the Hivers have internal communication provides another source of hope. If the Hivers communicate internally, perhaps humans can learn this language. But these are possibilities only hinted at in this novel, and McCaffrey's reader can only hope that she will return to this series soon and further explore the ramifications of an alien species dominated by its females.

What does the series as a whole communicate? Because the main characters are all from a single family, the series can be read as a science fiction soap opera as we follow the trials and tribulations of a powerful and Talented family. But McCaffrey complicates this simple plot by using this family and their adventures to raise important social and ethical issues. As in her other novels, this series poignantly depicts the difficulties faced by individuals who are gifted and different from their fellows. Having Talent does not mean that Rowan and her family can be tyrannical or make decisions for others. Instead their Talent puts them at the service of other humans, and creates social and psychological hardships for them. To rise above such difficulties requires Rowan and her family to be especially tolerant and open-minded. Their reward for such attitudes are the thrill of encountering the other, of bridging the gap between human and alien and the gaps created by prejudice about race and sexual orientation. The lively and likeable characters that McCaffrey creates are likely to make her readers see the disadvantages of narrow and parochial beliefs and the advantages of tolerance.

ALTERNATE READING: MARXIST

A Marxist approach to *The Rowan* series would examine the structures of power and commercialism revealed in the novel. Karl Marx's writings predict a social revolution based on economic differences and conflict among classes of people: the working class, the middle class, and the ruling class. A Marxist view of the world stresses the ways that the wealthy exploit and dehumanize the working class. Karl Marx described capitalism as a corrupt class system in which only those who owned the means of production exercised any actual political or economic power. Writing in the mid-nineteenth century, Marx believed that the working class would soon rise up against the middle and ruling classes. This revolution never occurred in the way that Marx envisioned it, but his ideas about class and economics have helped historians and literary critics analyze culture. Literary Marxism examines the ways in which writers reflect aspects of the class struggle that is based on economic differences.

A Marxist approach might emphasize McCaffrey's writings in terms of their position as bestsellers, as material objects that have a particular function in a particular historical period. Books, like other parts of culture, contain ideology, or a set of cultural beliefs. A Marxist could analyze *The Rowan* series to see what it reveals about economic and other attitudes. In *The Rowan* series McCaffrey displays a keen interest in economic considerations, and in her construction of societies on other worlds, she always takes account of economic incentives and effects. In *The Rowan* series, McCaffrey sharply criticizes the ways that corporations exploit individuals and dehumanize them.

Rigorously trained by another Talent to develop her skills, Rowan works for Federated Telepath and Telekinetic, a corporation that moves people and objects throughout a nine-planet system. As the corporation's name suggests, FT&T is a huge monopoly, one that pays its Talents well, but a company that also exploits the Talents. In the short story that introduces us to Rowan, McCaffrey describes Talents as "golden geese" for FT&T. Every Talent, but most especially the Primes, are overworked. Because Primes are so rare, they never get to take vacations or even leave their posts. Alternately cosseted and cajoled, the Talents move goods through space, keeping a huge economy going. The Talents operate, but do not own the means of production. Similarly, *The Rowan* series reifies the idea that the special individual will rise to the top of the social structure. The dominance of FT&T is never questioned, by the Talents or by the reader. Rowan's naivete about greed reinforces this view: "Not being of an acquisitive nature, she also did not understand the economics involved" (177). Her husband's colony, Deneb, is deeply in debt to Central Worlds and Rowan does what she can to improve the colony's financial and material standing. Even the disastrous mud slide that destroyed an entire community, except for Rowan, might have been avoided, except for the pressures of capitalist economics. The directors of the company that owned Rowan Mining Camp had debated evacuating the camp, but decided against the measure because the camp was just beginning to turn a profit (8). McCaffrey reveals just enough of the damage caused by the capitalistic structure to make the reader realize how damaging debt and profit systems can be.

Similarly, in *Pegasus in Flight*, McCaffrey exposes the exploitation of workers, Talented and unTalented, in the building of the space platform. Eager to meet or exceed the schedule in order to make a profit, the builders try to force Talents to work in stressful and debilitating conditions. Far worse is their treatment of unskilled workers from the slums. Proper protection is not provided for workers and many drift away to die in space; no attempt is made to rescue them and their suits have no radios to call for help. The Talents, however, change this situation by using their mental powers to locate and rescue the abandoned workers.

Similarly, Rowan's and other Talents' loneliness and alienation reveal how the Talent parallels the worker in a Marxist analysis. Rowan's "bitter, screaming loneliness" (*The Rowan* 151) is a high price to pay for her job. Exploited and manipulated by FT&T, Talents have no option but to work for the corporation. Alienated from their work, they frequently characterize themselves as space stevedores, moving material through space, an unglamorous profession at best. While the Talents are essential to the functioning of FT&T, as all workers are, McCaffrey does not show Talents making decisions or owning the means of production. Instead the characters do not challenge or question their jobs, even though they receive very little time off and they have difficulty finding and developing personal lives. It takes Jeff Raven, the untrained Talent from Deneb, to point out to Rowan that "FT&T of yours has exploited you for such a long time that you've never stopped to realize that you, as a Prime AND a citizen of Central Worlds have certain inalienable rights" (193). The Talents thus function as versions of the hero in an Horatio Alger story, gifted and destined to rise to the top. But while Horatio Alger uncritically depicts the possible rise to the top of a social structure, McCaffrey depicts its cost to the individual. *The Rowan* series, then, reflects the capitalistic culture that it was written in, but like all such texts the series also reveals tensions and resistance to the glorification of capitalism.

7

The Planet Pirate Series

The Planet Pirate series demonstrates Anne McCaffrey's remarkable creativity and resilience as a writer. Begun in 1978 with *Dinosaur Planet*, this series includes a number of remarkable innovations in science fiction. First, well before Michael Crichton capitalized on the popularity of dinosaurs with *Jurassic Park*, McCaffrey creates a believable setting in which Earth dinosaurs still roam on another planet. Second, McCaffrey demonstrates the power and originality of her concept of human explorers dealing with a planet of dinosaurs by continuing the series, not only with her own *Dinosaur Planet Survivors* (1984), but also in three subsequent novels written with two different co-authors: *Sassinak* written with Elizabeth Moon (1990); *The Death of Sleep* written with Jody Lynn Nye (1990); and *Generation Warriors* with Elizabeth Moon (1991). The dates of the books alone indicate both McCaffrey's extraordinary productivity—she was writing volumes in a number of other series at this same time—and her generosity in "sharing her universe," a science fiction writing pattern discussed in greater detail in Chapter 2.

Unlike *The Doona* series (see Chapter 9), *The Planet Pirate* series expands rather than contracts McCaffrey's vision. While in *The Doona* series the subsequent books seem merely to repeat the plot of the first book, in *The Planet Pirate* series the books expand the themes and characters of the first book. As this chapter will demonstrate, *The Planet Pirate* series uses a few main characters to explore issues that are central to all of Mc-

Caffrey's work. Co-authoring here builds on McCaffrey's strengths and develops the series in such a way that the reader feels continuity of narrative line and theme. This success is a tribute not only to McCaffrey, but also to her two co-authors. While it is impressive when two writers collaborate, when three work together closely and achieve such a seamless and enjoyable text as *The Planet Pirate* series, the accomplishment is all the more remarkable. In a way, the authors set up a paradigm parallel to their cooperation within the series, because the women characters also work closely together to achieve a difficult goal. One of the themes of the series is the importance of cooperation and working together.

Elizabeth Moon, who co-wrote two of the volumes with McCaffrey, is herself a writer of some reknown. Born 19 years after McCaffrey, Moon made her reputation as a writer of fantasy for her trilogy *The Deed of Paskennarion*. A skilled and polished stylist, Moon's tendency toward fantasy suggests again the primacy of McCaffrey's contribution to their collaborations, because *The Planet Pirate* series is clearly science fiction with more than a hint of space opera. "Space opera" is the term that describes action-adventure stories set in a science fiction setting and frequently involving wars between different species. Generously, McCaffrey describes her experience of working with Moon: "My partner in the enterprise had areas of competence and/or knowledge which I did not. Elizabeth Moon was a captain of Marines and had first-hand experience with military training, which we used to advantage in *Sassinak* and *Generation Warriors*, even though Sassinak was originally my character. Elizabeth IMPROVED her tremendously" (E-mail message, 3-9-95). McCaffrey demonstrates a generosity of spirit surely paralleled by the characters in these novels, Lunize and Sassinak. Unlike Moon, Jody Lynn Nye does not even have an entry in *The Science Fiction Encyclopedia*, but she is a long-time collaborator with McCaffrey; their first grand venture being Nye's *The Dragonlover's Guide to Pern* (1989), in which Nye introduces and explains Pern (see Chapters 3 and 4).

Perhaps because McCaffrey so carefully delineates the characters and situations in the first two books, those that follow six and seven years later continue the themes that are McCaffrey's trademarks: strong admirable female heroines; original and thought-provoking science fiction settings and problems; ethical issues and dilemmas; exciting and engaging plots. Along the way, McCaffrey and her co-authors raise issues of racism, genetic ethics, sexism, and animal rights.

PLOT DEVELOPMENT

Dinosaur Planet

Set in the same universe of Federated Sentient Planets as most of McCaffrey's other novels, *Dinosaur Planet* follows the adventures of a mixed-race crew sent to explore and evaluate the planet Ireta. Their mission—to catalogue Ireta's flora and fauna and search for energy sources—is a standard one. But as one might expect from a writer of McCaffrey's originality and creativity, the plot is anything but standard science fiction. Well-delineated characters and thought-provoking situations make the difference between stereotypical science fiction and McCaffrey's finely crafted tales.

The plot pits the lightweights—Lunzie, Varian, and Kai—against the heavyworlders. The entire crew is troubled by their lack of contact with the ship that left them on Ireta. The heavyworlders believe that the crew has been "planted" or abandoned on the planet. The heavyworlders revert to savagery, as evidenced by their secretive meat-eating and hunting, and rebel against Vai and Karian's joint leadership. McCaffrey provides little sympathy and no point of view of the heavyworlders; instead we identify and sympathize with the lightweights, who barely escape with their lives, and who end the novel in a chemically induced sleep as they await rescue.

Dinosaur Planet Survivors

As its title suggests, this novel follows what happens when the survivors awaken, an incredible 43 years after the events of *Dinosaur Planet*. The survivors had hoped for rescue from their base ship, the ARCT-10, in months, not decades. But the ARCT-10 doesn't return at all; instead, a Thek, an alien species, wakens Kai who then rouses the other survivors. The Thek are a huge rock-like species, known for their immensely long lives and brevity of speech: "a form of granite with a nuclear core for energy" (17). Tremendously powerful, they rarely interfere in human affairs. Because of their virtual immortality, the Thek experience time differently than humans. To the Thek, the humans seem very ephemeral and their problems of little importance. Throughout *The Dinosaur Planet* series, however, they make critical interventions, such as their awakening of Kai.

The ARCT-10 is missing in a cosmic storm, and during the 43-year absence the heavyworlders have produced two generations of descendents. So Kai, Varian, and Lunzie must figure out how to protect themselves, Ireta, and the planet's remarkable flora and fauna from the heavyworlders' attempts to claim it. They do so in part by establishing the right of the developing intelligent life forms to their own planet and by discovering how dinosaurs came to Ireta. The Thek owe a debt to Ireta, because it is one of their preserves. The Thek had a previous history (unknown to humans) of pillaging planets for energy; eons ago, in an attempt to rectify their environmentally disastrous consumption, a Thek took dinosaurs and other life forms from Earth and transplanted them to Ireta. Ireta, then, is a wildlife preserve. Varian and Kai decide to stay there to look after it. Their decision is enforced by a Thek conference, and by the arrival of Sassinak, a Fleet captain. (The Fleet is the military arm of Federated Sentient Planets.) Because of the time paradox of cold-sleep—those in coldsleep do not age—Sassinak turns out to be Lunzie's great-great-great granddaughter.

The arrival of Sassinak and her ship connects the first two books with the last three books. As McCaffrey does in her other series, here she tells a narrative from two perspectives. In *Dinosaur Planet Survivors*, we meet Sassinak and see the events through Lunzie's eyes. Then, in the second half of *Sassinak* (book three), some of the same events are told from Sassinak's point of view. This doubled perspective allows McCaffrey and her co-author to comment on the interpretation of events and the importance of point of view. A pleasurable repetition, these sections are only part of longer histories of the characters. The similarities and differences between Lunzie and Sassinak create a complex relationship, another example of McCaffrey's ability to create believable and fascinating characters. The overlap also generates cogent and compelling bridges between the books in the series. Reading *Sassinak* after *Dinosaur Planet Survivors*, the reader cannot easily tell that six years have passed between their publication dates.

Sassinak

Sassinak follows the title character from childhood up to her meeting with her ancestor Lunzie on Ireta. An engrossing bildungsroman (novel of development), *Sassinak* explains how and why the title character became a Fleet captain. Like Lunzie and the other Dinosaur Planet survivors, Sassinak's life has been altered by the pirating planets. While Lunzie and her companions lose 43 years of time, Sassinak loses all her family and friends when planet pirates attack her colony world. Enslaved, Sassinak becomes a pilot flying for the pirates, and she meets an older man, Abe, who rescues her. A Fleet enlisted man, Abe adopts Sassinak and encourages her to join the Fleet Academy, which she does. On the night of her graduation Abe is murdered by someone hired by planet pirates, so Sassinak adopts the Fleet as her family and home. Her solitude makes Sassinak's discovery of Lunzie and their relationship all the more poignant. Sassinak's ship provides the crucial intervention in saving the crew, but most of this novel focuses on Sassinak's development. At the end of the book, Sassinak offers Lunzie a position on her ship, and Lunzie eagerly accepts.

The Death of Sleep

This book's title points to the terrible tragedy inherent in a number of coldsleeps. While coldsleep is used only in emergency situations, Lunzie encounters such emergencies three times. Because of her extended coldsleeps, Lunzie loses her daughter, who dies before Lunzie can contact her. As *The Death of Sleep* shows, Lunzie's history is just as fascinating as Sassinak's. The fourth book in the series provides an explanation for Lunzie's mysteriousness. A woman out of time, she has endured two rare extended bouts of coldsleep—once for over 60 years and once for a decade, both before the 43 years that she remains in suspended animation on Ireta. In all three instances, emergencies beyond her control make coldsleep her only option. The plot focuses on how Lunzie copes with such adverse circumstances. Her adventures are just as exciting as Sassinak's, but they emphasize psychological trauma more than adventure with aliens and the military.

Generation Warriors

The most recent, but hopefully not the last, in the series, *Generation Warriors* combines the focus on Lunzie and Sassinak in the two preceding books. The two women combine forces and succeed in exposing the corporate and family connections that have enabled planet pirates to prey on helpless colonies. The events of the book pick up where *Sassinak* ends—with Lunzie joining Sassinak's crew. Their close sympathy is emphasized through similar gestures and a sense that they have an almost telepathic communication. But each must fight planet pirates in her own way: Sassinak commands a ship and then leads a planetary rebellion; Lunzie travels to the heavyworld home planet and discovers the connection with planet pirates. In her struggle, Lunzie learns to sympathize with heavyworlders, so much so that she represents their point of view to the Thek, who hold a conference that is the human equivalent of a trial. While Lunzie and Sassinak ultimately succeed in their mission, they also learn to let go of their need for vengeance and to understand the perspectives of those different from them. Here McCaffrey and Nye separate their books from those of other, more simple-minded space operas.

The plot contains two separate story lines: Sassinak's and Lunzie's. Each story line follows one character and her adventures. Sassinak must struggle in space, as the captain, to fight against the infiltration and corruption that enable the planet pirates to thrive. Lunzie, on the other hand, must face the heavyworlders and their culture. She searches for clues and allies on the heavyworld planet and confronts old friends. At the end, the two story lines are integrated as Sassinak's and Lunzie's world coalesce. Together, they have the knowledge and power to expose the planet pirates and their allies.

CHARACTER DEVELOPMENT

Dinosaur Planet and *Dinosaur Planet Survivors*

On the exploration team depicted in *Dinosaur Planet* some members of the crew are ship-bred, some planet-bred, but the biggest difference lies between "heavyworlder" humans who come from Diplo, a planet with higher-than-Earth gravity, and the lighter weight humans who come from Earth. Living on Diplo has caused genetic mutations in the heavyworlders, including "heavy" or well-developed musculature. Heavyworlders have a long and complex history of dealing with prejudice and abandonment by companies in Federated Sentient Planets, but that history is only alluded to in *Dinosaur Planet*. The prejudice that heavyworlders face does, however, have consequences. In part because of their history, the heavyworlders mutiny, try to kill all the other humans, whom they call "lightweights," and endeavor to claim Ireta as a colony planet for heavyworlders.

The mutiny of heavyworlders dominates *Dinosaur Planet*, the first book in the series, and shapes the events of the other four novels. The heavyworlders are despised by lightweights because of the heavyworlders' regressive culture and their perceived brutishness. With their extreme musculature, heavy bodies, and shorter lifespans, the heavyworlders in turn resent the lightweights, who eschew meat-eating for ethical reasons. "A civilized diet no longer included animal flesh" (7) readers are told in *Dinosaur Planet*. Off Diplo, heavyworlders also refrain from meat-eating, but when they were originally left on Diplo without appropriate communications they had been forced to eat meat and use leather, and they continue the practice as part of their cultural difference. Such physical and cultural differences cause great animosity between the heavyworld and lightweight members of the crew, and inspired by the dinosaurs' carnivorous habits on Ireta, the heavyworlders begin to eat meat there, an action connected to their decision to kill the rest of the exploratory team and claim Ireta as a heavyworld colony.

The overt connection between flesh-eating and mutiny and the evolution of most other species away from meat consumption in *Dinosaur Planet* comments negatively on our own carnivorous behavior. In this series, by definition, meat-eating is regressive, in part because of some animal life's potential for sentience. Mary Brizzi argues that "the vegetarian ethic of the novel may leave some readers dissatisfied" (*Anne McCaffrey* 73), and even comments on the novel's "vegetarian bias" (74), but McCaffrey uses vegetarianism to raise larger issues about ethics and cultural difference. As animal rights become more of an issue of our world, McCaffrey looks less like a biased writer than a prescient one.

Ireta contains remarkable specimens of dinosaur life, some of it apparently intelligent—hence the novel's name, *Dinosaur Planet*. Members of the crew are fascinated by the behavior and size of the animals especially, and puzzled by what the presence of Earth creatures means on a planet so very far from Earth. By creating a world populated by dinosaurs, McCaffrey raises issues of predator and victim and of evolution. Both repulsed and attracted by the brutal violence of the dinosaurs, the crew find in the creatures a chance to examine human behavior and social mores. The heavyworlders find in the dinosaurs a model and justification for their brutal behavior. The unaltered lightweight humans, however, find most of the dinosaurs and their brutality troubling.

The novel presents these actions from the perspective of three lightweights, the co-leaders of the crew: Varian, a female xenobiologist with a specialty in animals; Kai, the male pilot; and Lunzie, the female medic. These characters' quick thinking and resourcefulness are all that stand between them and death during the mutiny. Varian and Kai are lovers and part of *Dinosaur Planet*, and especially *Dinosaur Planet Survivors* deal with the very adult theme of how to work and manage a relationship simultaneously.

Like Varian, Lunzie demonstrates unusual and admirable physical endurance and strength of character. In *Dinosaur Planet*, Lunzie is something of a mysterious figure, aloof and somehow different. She seems set apart because she is an Adept at an exercise called Discipline, training that allows a human to behave with superhuman endurance and strength for short periods of time. While not as advanced as Lunzie, Varian also has training in Discipline. That the characters who excel in Discipline are usually female suggests again McCaffrey's interest in creating powerful and extraordinary female characters.

Lunzie holds the series together, as a pivotal character in four of the five books in the series. Lunzie has had previously both positive and negative experiences with heavyworlders, but this mutiny strongly tests her ability to judge fairly. Part of the series focuses on the issue of racial division, and Lunzie's eventual defeat of racial prejudice shows that McCaffrey and her co-authors believe that physical and cultural difference can and must be overcome. But these issues are fully developed only through the whole series; at the end of *Dinosaur Planet*, the mutineers have apparently succeeded in taking over Ireta, and Lunzie places herself and the other survivors in coldsleep, or chemically-induced suspended animation, to await rescue. Ironically, humans' coldsleep raises important questions about dinosaurs: Were they cold or warm blooded? What part did this factor play in their dominance of the Earth for millions of years and their eventual extinction? While these questions are not resolved, the mystery of the dinosaurs' appearance on Ireta is—in the next book. For these humans stranded on Ireta, the coldbloodedness of coldsleep provides the only way to survive.

Sassinak

A superb tactician, Sassinak moves up the ranks to become the captain of her own ship, with a mission to ferret out planet pirates as well as the companies and wealthy families that enable the pirates to exist. The courage and skill that Sassinak demonstrates are emphasized by the prominence of Rudyard Kipling as the Fleet's adopted poet laureate. Frequent citations of Kipling and his words connect the second half of the series, setting an adventurous tone. For example, as Sassinak and Lunzie celebrate their discovery of each other, Sassinak recites a long section of Kipling's "L 'Envoi," which includes a line about travelling fastest alone. Lunzie questions Sassinak about that poem and about her family. Art thus provides a means for Lunzie to ask difficult questions and to get to know Sassinak better. The poem enables Sassinak to explain her feelings through art, and Sassinak's quotation prompts Lunzie's tactful questioning. Both Sassinak and Lunzie have been forced by tragedy to travel alone—until they find each other. In addition to their common interest in language, Sassinak, like Lunzie, practices Discipline, but she is a more active and literally commanding figure than Lunzie.

The Death of Sleep

Lunzie's bravery and longevity in enduring coldsleep make her the expert on the phenomenon. Like Ripley in *Aliens* (as described in the novelization of James Cameron's film), Lunzie is separated from and loses her daughter during her first and second coldsleeps. Like Ripley, Lunzie takes a job with a mining company ship expecting to be away for only a couple of years. But the greed and bad management of the corporation break the most important of all bonds, the mother-daughter tie. Also like *Aliens*, *The Death of Sleep* uses family ties to emphasize how inhumane corporate practices are. As with Ripley, Lunzie possesses instincts that should be heeded, but are not, with disastrous consequences for her and the other passengers. McCaffrey and Nye also emphasize the importance of feminine qualities when they have Lunzie confront the changes in medicine that occur during her first coldsleep. After the 62 years, medicine now emphasizes diagnosis almost exclusively through machines, and in her retraining Lunzie argues for the importance of touch and person-to-person contact. "Too much of the real work of the physician had been taken out of the hands of the practitioner and placed in the 'hands' of cold, impersonal machines" (67). Lunzie argues with her professor: " 'But what about a patient's feelings? The mood and mental condition of your patient are as important as the scientific treatment available for his ailment' " (67–68). That Lunzie argues with a male professor underscores the traditionally feminine aspect of her argument. As in much science fiction, the issue can be directly applied to current situations in medicine. Lunzie courageously enters this brave new world of even more dependence on technology, and the novel closes with her being forced to enter coldsleep on Ireta.

THEMES

Racism and the Necessity of Tolerance: The Wefts

To succeed in their mission to defeat piracy, Sassinak, like Lunzie, must overcome prejudice—not only against heavyworlders but also against the shape-changing Wefts, aliens who assume human form to work with the human Fleet. Much like Odo on *Star-Trek: Deep Space Nine*, the Wefts have a completely nonhumanoid form and alien sexuality. In their natural form they have many tentacles and a fearful shape. They mate only in groups in their home ocean. Their metamorphic and telepathic abilities make them classic female aliens (See Chapter 2), and as a result, they are feared and despised by many humans. The Weft make superb warriors because their shape-shifting abilities enable them to move at superhuman speed and through any barrier.

While a cadet at Fleet Academy (in *Sassinak*), Sassinak befriends a Weft and defends it and other Weft cadets against an unjust accusation of stealing. Her open-mindedness and fairness provide Sassinak with Weft friends for life. Valuable allies and bodyguards because of their shape-changing and telepathic abilities, the Wefts save Sassinak's life on a number of occasions. Like Lunzie, Sassinak also makes great efforts not to judge heavyworlders based on prejudice against them. Because of her experience in slavery, Sassinak persuades the heavyworlders at the Fleet Academy that she'll be fair to them. She will make a good captain because of her "unusual ability to make friends with people of all backgrounds" (*Sassinak* 49). Her willingness to communicate with another alien in its larval form, a Ssli, also saves her life and her crew's in *Generation Warriors*.

The Ssli

The Ssli are another of McCaffrey and Nye's original contributions to science fiction aliens, and they too serve to reveal the stupidity of racism.

A telepathic race that has a larval stage, some individual Ssli work as astrogaters (navigators through the stars) on Fleet ships. A particular Ssli remembers Sassinak's courtesy to it, and uses its telepathic abilities to warn her of an invasion. This pattern begins in *Dinosaur Planet* where Varian, the xenobiologist, bonds with the giffs, flying dinosaurs, who then protect Varian, Lunzie, and the others through their long coldsleep. Throughout this series and McCaffrey's fiction in general, open-mindedness is invariably rewarded in a spectacular fashion. McCaffrey uses science fiction tropes to argue for tolerance and the importance of respecting difference.

Genetics and Ethics

Throughout the series, ethical issues are raised about genetic altera-tions to humans. The Seti, a violent and carnivorous race, claim to feel sympathy for the heavyworlders, seeing them as victims in a genetic experiment. The heavyworlders believe that Federated Sentient Planets may "plant" or abandon humans on worlds to see what happens. Even Varian and Kai, the leaders of the team attacked by their heavyworld colleagues, briefly consider that their team may have been abandoned. Varian and Kai see that the heavyworlders believe, based on the history of Diplo's abandonment, that their team has been "planted" on Ireta.

The notion of "planting" raises questions such as: Is it right to alter humans to adapt to a planet? One complication to this question occurs when the heavyworlders' descendents turn out to be quite appealing. After their 43-year coldsleep, Varian finds herself attracted to Aygar, one of the original mutineers' descendents. Varian, Lunzie, and Sassinak all find Aygar an attractive and compelling presence. Because Aygar is su-premely fit and intelligent, they all see in him a positive benefit of ad-aptation. It is his speed, strength, and intelligence that save Sassinak's life more than once in *Generation Warriors*. His character and the three women's attraction to him seem to suggest as well that some connection to animal nature may be beneficial and justified by necessity, as it is for Aygar, raised on Ireta, a dangerous world without high technology.

Art and Tolerance

Lunzie attends an art performance that encapsulates the pain and suf-fering of the heavyworlders. She finds the opera *Bitter Destiny* moving and quite unlike lightweight art. McCaffrey describes the opera as "that absolutely marvelous bit" and credits Moon with adding it to their book. (E-mail 4-12-95) As part of the performance, the audience actually engages in sexual intercourse—their seats even recline to facilitate their participation. The activity takes place as the opera depicts the first colonists' decision to survive by reproducing and saving women and children at the expense of the men. The reenactment stresses the importance of those acts of reproduction. The act seems bizarre to Lunzie, and she cannot participate anyway because of the suit she wears to protect her body from Diplo's heavy gravity. But through this experience, Lunzie realizes how strongly the heavyworlders feel about their history. The opera, along with her relationship with Zebara, a heavyworlder she knew and admired before her extended coldsleep, enables her to overcome her prejudice and the suffering heavyworlders caused her. Although Lunzie does not share the heavyworlders' history, after she witnesses their art she can understand their point of view. McCaffrey and her co-authors' view of heavyworlders and animals presents the animalistic side of humanity with sympathy, implying that cultural and physical difference should not present insuperable barriers. As McCaffrey makes clear in her other series, especially *The Dragonriders of Pern*, *The Brain Ship* series, and *The Crystal Singer* series, art, such as the heavyworld opera performance—*or* science fiction novels like McCaffrey's—can provide a way to explore difference and stress the importance of tolerance.

Animal Rights

The connection of the heavyworlders to the beauty and potential of dinosaurs is quite explicit, raising the issue of animal rights along with the issue of genetic alteration. The dinosaurs have been "planted" on Ireta by the Theks to preserve them from extinction. The Theks, in part, are attempting to rectify errors they made, when, energy-crazy, they stripped whole planets of life. Varian explains the appeal of the winged dinosaurs by suggesting they represent "the freedom, or perhaps the view, the perspective, the feeling of infinite space around you" (*Dinosaur Planet* 117). While the winged dinosaurs represent one appeal, the "fang face," or Tyrannosaurus rex, represents another facet of human nature, one less appealing. As the heavyworlders mutiny, one of them is described with "an expression close to the snarl of a fang face" (*Dinosaur*

Planet 176). The carnivorous behavior and predatory instincts of the heavyworlders are revealed as they imitate the Tyrannosaurus rex and hunt other dinosaurs to eat their flesh. While this behavior is depicted as regressive, it is because humans have evolved beyond flesh-eating. Animals do, however, retain qualities that are admirable and should be respected.

In *Dinosaur Planet Survivors*, Varian the xenobiologist expresses a preference for the openness and honesty of animals versus the duplicity of humans. To Lunzie she explains, "I've generally dealt with animals which are pretty straightforward in their reactions. I really feel sorry for you having to cope with that devious and subtle predator—man" (55). What a crew member says about the appeal of dinosaurs also applies to the heavyworlders: "Dinosaurs are big, they're ugly, and they're fascinating. Raw power, a force of nature, majestic" (276). Lunzie herself feels this appeal when she meets Zebara, a heavyworlder whom she knew and was attracted to decades ago. Even as an old man, huge and ugly, he still exudes a physical attraction for her, and their relationship allows her to carry data back to the Federated Planets trial that exposes the planet pirates and their connection with the heavyworlders. At the same time, Lunzie's experiences enable her to defend and justify the heavyworlders' actions. At the trial, she defends them so ably, fully understanding their culture, that they are not punished as the Seti, the other planet pirate allies, are.

In an almost parallel situation to Lunzie's defense of the heavyworlders, the planet Ireta is protected because of the intelligence of the beautiful and attractive giffs (pteranodons) and the rapacious and frightening fringes (like mossy octupi and alien—not dinosaur-like at all), which attack humans, because both species manifest intelligence. We should choose to respect animals, the authors seem to be saying, not based on the appeal or similar values of animals, but on whether they have the potential to develop sentience. Understanding why the fringes attack humans makes it possible to understand and to forgive, as understanding the heavyworlders' culture allows Lunzie to explain and to sympathize with their actions.

Sexism

In addition to racism and animal rights, this series also directly addresses feminist issues. By exploring the difficulties that the female characters have because of their sex, emphasizing the relationships between women, and creating strong female heroines, McCaffrey and her co-authors alter the traditional emphasis in science fiction on male characters and a masculine ethos in each novel in *The Planet Pirate* series. (See Chapter 2 for more discussion of women and science fiction.) The female character Varian works as a co-leader with Kai in *Dinosaur Planet* and *Dinosaur Planet Survivors*, and she struggles with the lack of respect she is accorded, especially by the heavyworlders, because she is female. Similarly, in *Generation Warriors* Lunzie discovers the explanation for the subordination of women on Diplo, the heavyworld planet; because of their altered physique, it is much harder for heavyworld women to bear children, so they are socialized to believe that they cannot have both careers and children. Like women in our history, heavyworld women are kept subordinate through an emphasis on childbearing to the exclusion of other activities. Lunzie's encounter with heavyworld women repeats the emphasis on heavyworlder society as regressive and more primitive than lightweight humanity. The subordination of women thus parallels the subordination and exploitation of animals.

The authors use gender role reversals to expose sexism. In *Dinosaur Planet Survivors*, Kai awakens Varian, and it is Varian who jokes about Sleeping Beauty and kisses him, a role reversal from the traditional fairy tale. In a similar role reversal, Varian remains strong and Kai is weakened by an attack by an alien. When Kai is attacked and severely injured by a fringe, Varian must worry about her relationship with him. In his weakened state, Kai seems less attractive than the exceptionally virile Aygar. Varian even worries that her sexual attraction to Aygar may distract her from her duties as co-leader of the exploration team. Although the conflict is resolved, it suggests the complexities and difficulties of being a co-leader while maintaining a sexual relationship. Like Varian, Sassinak (in *Sassinak*) also must confront conflicts between her command position and her lover Huron, who loses his life fighting planet pirates. Both women learn to respect their mates' decisions, and neither abuses her power as leader.

Repeated references in the last three books to a video heroine emphasize the messiness of real-life command. As a child Sassinak identifies with Carin Coldae, a video heroine who has incredible adventures in space, but who never loses her beauty or physical appeal. In fact, Coldae never even musses her hair. The glamorization of Coldae suggests the unreality of femininity as a construct—gorgeous appearance and sex appeal must be maintained despite the most horrific of circumstances.

McCaffrey and Nye and Moon also suggest the fictiveness of femininity—Coldae is an unreal and unattainable role model. That the actual woman who played Coldae and her fan clubs turn out to have been fundraising for a racist terrorist cult (*Sassinak* 249–250) suggests again the danger of believing in images. In a comment that could apply to fiction in general, McCaffrey and Nye may be slyly teasing their readers. Sassinak tells a young would-be freedom fighter: "I had a Coldae poster, in silver, when I was a girl. But that was a picture. Reality's different" (*Generation Warriors* 286). "Reality" appears in science fiction indirectly, as it does in the depiction of sexism faced by Sassinak and Lunzie. In both instances, McCaffrey and Nye point to the ways that experiences are represented falsely.

Sassinak discovers that the life of a real female Fleet officer in space is far more complicated than that depicted in the videos she saw as a girl. When abducted by slavers, Sassinak faces the prospect of being forced into prostitution. There are pressures on poor women especially to become prostitutes, and like Sassinak, who is protected by Abe, many women are only one man away from selling their bodies as prostitutes or in marriage. "Civilized" society also contains sexism as Sassinak realizes when she encounters sexual harassment while at the Fleet Academy. A child of an influential family, later implicated in planet piracy, tries to force Sassinak to have sex with him. She risks expulsion and discipline when she resists his advances. While the authors expose sexism, they also provide alternatives. Sassinak also learns from a female admiral who teaches her about command presence, in a special class for women officers. "It's not your size or your looks or your strength or how loud you can yell—it's something *else*, inside" (7) the admiral tells the young female cadets. The message that sexism exists, but that it can and should be resisted, makes Sassinak a valuable female role model.

In a complementary fashion, Lunzie's experience reveals the sexism that single mothers face as they struggle to earn a living and raise a family. Lunzie's original coldsleep of 62 years occurs when, as a single mother, she must leave her daughter to take a job at a mining colony. Lunzie misses most of her daughter's life. Her daughter is still alive after Lunzie awakens and she takes another job as a medic on a luxury ship that will take her to her daughter's planet. However, because of the corporation's failure to maintain the ship properly, Lunzie ends up in coldsleep again when the ship malfunctions—this time for over 10 years, thus missing her daughter's life completely. This cruel irony underscores the tremendous cost to mothers and daughters of a system that emphasizes profit over safety and family. While Lunzie misses her daughter's life, she is able to help another female relative who is trapped by the conservatism of her family. Lunzie gives Lona the money for a stake in a mining colony, enabling this distant relative of hers, a spirited young woman, the means to escape her family. These examples of sexism and women helping other women appear throughout the series, a constant reminder of the importance of female solidarity. Most significantly, such help occurs over generational splits, suggesting that female solidarity can overcome historical differences. In Lunzie's case, she is able to overcome over 100 years of time, again evoking Sleeping Beauty's 100-year sleep as Varian and Kai do in *Dinosaur Planet Survivors*. And Lunzie finds particular and unique fulfillment, not granted *Aliens'* Ripley, of discovering the life of her descendents many generations later.

Despite sexism and the obstacles placed by time, McCaffrey's female characters invariably succeed. Sassinak even wrests an acknowledgment of her superior intelligence from a Security officer hidden on her staff. Marooned with dangerous aliens, almost killed by pirates, Dupaynil, the Security officer, says to Sassinak's second in command: "The worst of it is it's all my fault for thinking I was smarter than your Sassinak" (*Generation Warriors* 335). Sassinak describes her situation in less than glowing terms: "a single Fleet captain against the most powerful families in the Federation, against the massed pirates, plus the Seti?" (283). But because of her ability to work with all kinds of people, including Aygar the heavyworld descendent, Wefts, Ssli, and the underground people she discovers, Sassinak does succeed against all odds. The emphasis on how relationship and cooperation lead to military victory is a twist on traditional science fiction space opera, which stresses individual heroics. Indeed, one reason for McCaffrey's appeal as a writer is her well-developed depiction of human relationships, especially those among women.

The relationships among the human females in the series are sophisticated and engaging. McCaffrey and her co-authors evoke the issues of co-authorship through a complex relationship between two of the main characters in the series: Lunzie and Sassinak. Through the device of cold-sleep, these two very distant relatives find themselves working together, generations apart, as "Generation Warriors," fighting planet pirates. Because Lunzie has already been in extended coldsleep before, she has outlived her child and her children's children. At the chronological age of 110, she is rescued by her great-great-great granddaughter, who looks like and has lived longer than Lunzie herself. Because of their similarity, the two women bond quickly, but they also must work through some important differences, because their life experiences vary. Sassinak has experienced planet pirates and slavery first-hand and is now a member of the military Fleet, while Lunzie, a medical officer, sees the world very differently. Lunzie also practices Discipline, an art akin to Tai Chi and Kung Fu, in which the practitioner can influence others and perform superhuman feats. Sassinak also has some experience with Discipline, but she relies more on her remarkable survival skills and a keen tactician's instinct for manipulation and strategy. Together the two must figure out how best to combine their skills to combat the scourge of planet piracy, which has changed and darkened both their lives.

Lunzie and Sassinak provide a parallel to the co-authoring of McCaffrey and Nye and McCaffrey and Moon. The complex working relationship of these two formidable female characters must surely reflect some of the difficulties faced by two writers, working together to create novels in a shared universe. The generational difference represented by coldsleep must affect McCaffrey's work with the younger, less experienced writers, too. The sympathetic depiction of the characters' working relationship suggests some of the affection and work and negotiating that must go on in co-authoring a book. And of course, the relationship can also function as a model for her readers who daily work in the real world with other women in important tasks—less glamorous than fighting planet pirates, perhaps, but still crucial work. By reading about Lunzie and Sassinak and Varian, McCaffrey's readers can take inspiration from their example of cooperation.

ALTERNATE READING: PSYCHOANALYTIC CRITICISM

Psychoanalytic criticism explores the parallels between the unconscious and fiction. Like dreams, a particular manifestation of the unconscious mind, fiction contains truth and ideas that are neither obvious nor self-evident. Both dreams and fiction must be interpreted. Drawing upon the writings of Sigmund Freud, critics have applied the discipline of psychology to fiction writing. In *The Interpretation of Dreams*, Freud describes concepts he uses to analyze dreams, and these concepts can also be used by literary critics. First, Freud identifies the idea of the unconscious, a part of the mind that we are not consciously aware of. Second, Freud theorizes that the unconscious contains repressed thoughts and ideas—ideas that are either upsetting or forbidden by our society. Third, Freud posits that all humans are sexual beings, and that many of our sexual thoughts and desires are repressed and end up in our unconscious. Understanding that the unconscious contains forbidden desires can help explain otherwise inexplicable human behavior. Freud often used psychology to explain physical illness that had no clearly identifiable physical cause. By uncovering unconscious thoughts and anxieties, Freud discovered, for example, the source of a nervous cough of one of his patients.

Literary critics can also "diagnose" using psychology in two ways. First, a critic can attempt to psychoanalyze a writer by looking at her fiction and at her biography. This older form of psychoanalytic criticism is no longer the dominant practice, but it can provide thought-provoking analysis for readers. By examining McCaffrey's life and *The Planet Pirate* series, a critic might conclude that McCaffrey uses the planet pirates and other male characters to express a desire to impress her own father, who as we know from the dedication to one of her novels, was a military man. McCaffrey might be vicariously using Sassinak to have the kind of adventures that as a woman growing up in the 1940s, she was denied. A psychoanalytic critic might also examine the relationships among female characters to see what they might reveal about McCaffrey's relationship with her mother. Does Lunzie's extended coldsleep reflect McCaffrey's fear of abandonment by her mother? Such an anxiety is part of the psychology of all children. Does the sexual competition created between a great-great-great-grandaughter and her ancestress reflect anxieties about a mother's sexuality, or in even more Freudian terms, a competition for the father's attention between a mother and a daughter? Science fiction allows a kind of literalization of psychoanalytic metaphors, because only in science fiction could a mother actually be younger than her daughter (because of coldsleep).

While analyzing McCaffrey's unconscious that might be reflected in her characters and plots is thought-provoking, a more worthwhile application of psychoanalytic criticism might be in terms of McCaffrey's readers. McCaffrey's fictions are tremendously popular. This success is due in part to how well written the novels are. But there must also be something in the ideas, the plots, that captures readers' imaginations. Like Mary Shelley, who turned her own anxieties about childbearing into the most successful science fiction novel of all time, *Frankenstein*, McCaffrey turns her fantasies and desires into fictions that appeal to millions of readers. While the dragons of Pern (see Chapters 3 and 4) might be said to be phallic symbols, or a representation of sexuality, the beings that represent sexuality in *The Planet Pirate* series would have to be the dinosaurs and by extension, the heavyworlders. Through both, McCaffrey represents our forbidden desire for blood and violence. The pursuit of the planet pirates can also represent a desire for domination, revenge, and control. Lunzie and Sassinak are justified in their need to punish and revenge themselves on the pirates who might represent some aspect of the self or society that readers wish to control. Even the name of the planet, Ireta, which means angry (Brizzi, *Anne McCaffrey* 73), points to this repressed side of human nature. While humans have been civilized into controlling violent actions and into becoming vegetarians, McCaffrey points to the fascination with large beasts who obey none of the conventions of civilization. Varian especially experiences the pull of forbidden sexual desires when she is drawn to Aygar, the heavyworld descendent, when she should remain loyal to Kai. Lunzie experiences the rise of the repressed most directly during the heavyworld opera. Art usually represents or functions as a vehicle for unconscious desires, but in heavyworld art the unconscious becomes conscious and explicit. Instead of being simply titillated by hints of sexuality in art, heavyworlders actually engage in sex during the performance. This action makes literal the unconscious process in some works of art.

Lunzie and Sassinak can also represent an idealized mother-daughter relationship, one in which the mother and daughter are able to function as equals. While in actual psychoanalytic theory a daughter must separate herself from her mother, here the separation occurs through the mechanism of coldsleep. But despite the decades of sleep, Lunzie still finds a daughter when she awakes. Because they are close to the same age physiologically, though not chronologically, Lunzie and Sassinak have an opportunity to recreate the dynamics of the mother-daughter tie, fulfilling their desire to have the mother always with the daughter. Psychoanalytically, McCaffrey's series appeals to readers because it allows her audience to express and find satisfaction in human desires and relationships that are impossible in the real world.

Restoree

Restoree (1967) occupies an important place in McCaffrey's canon, and not only because it is her first published novel. The novel has gained considerable critical attention and is still in print almost 30 years later. Mary Brizzi describes *Restoree*'s unique features by claiming, "One thing is certain—*Restoree* is like no other science-fiction novel ever published" (*Anne McCaffrey* 12). The critical controversy about the book focuses on whether the novel parodies science fiction or is intended seriously. The plot follows the adventures of a young woman abducted by aliens who intend to eat her; she is rescued after being skinned alive by an evil scientist from another alien species, who restores her with a new beautiful skin and new facial features. This might seem like a heroic action by the scientist, except that the scientist rescues these victims only to experiment on them and turn them into slaves. The heroine Sara subsequently rescues an important and handsome political and war leader, and they fall in love. The story reads like an episode from a pulp science fiction magazine or from the popular cult television series, *The X-Files*. One of McCaffrey's notable qualities is that she creates or prepares for trends; in *Restoree*, McCaffrey designs a bizarre and unusual plot that is only now becoming more accepted.

PLOT DEVELOPMENT

Even if it were not an unusual and fascinating text, *Restoree* would still deserve attention as McCaffrey's first novel. It contains many qualities that feature prominently in her later fictions: a strong female protagonist, an original contribution to science fiction tropes, a semi-feudal culture with high and low technological features, the use of crystals for technology, and conflict and cooperation between alien species. At the same time, *Restoree* employs a standard science fiction scenario, the alien abduction. Sara Fulton has led a life of quiet desperation on Earth; rather unattractive and bullied by her family, Sara seems to have been a loner and she doesn't regret leaving Earth. In this regard, *Restoree* prefigures James Tiptree Jr.'s famous story, "The Women Men Don't See," in which two women voluntarily leave Earth with aliens because they find their position as women on Earth is so terrible. Sara is "a woman men don't see," and like the mother in Tiptree's story, Sara too is a librarian, quiet and unnoticed.

In Medias Res (beginning in the middle)

McCaffrey manipulates the reader into the plot by beginning *in medias res*, or in the middle. This Latin phrase describes a classic strategy used in epic poems to get the reader's attention. McCaffrey uses this technique to draw us into *Restoree*. The novel opens with Sara, a victim of amnesia—she doesn't know where she is or how she got there. The other people expect her to continue in her role as drudge and caretaker for a man who seems to be an idiot, but who turns out to be drugged into a barely functioning state. How did Sara get in this position? Who is the man she is nursing? What should she do to escape? These questions are raised by Sara's increasing awareness and knowledge about her situation. Like *Dragonflight* (see Chapter 3), *Restoree*'s plot presents readers with a mystery that they are eager to solve.

Mystery of "Restoration"

What is a "restoree"? This intriguing made-up word describes a unique and horrible experience—that of being skinned alive and being restored to life. But we don't know that this happened to Sara—and neither does she until almost halfway into the novel. This suspense adds to the reader's interest in the plot. Because the novel is told in first person, we identify with Sara, the narrator, and we are concerned as she is, about her abduction and mysterious reincarnation. While being restored seems awful, Sara is quite satisfied with her new body, which is far more attractive than her original body. Sara thus lives a fantasy of a complete makeover, the transformation from an ugly duckling into a swan. This kind of change can only be believable in a science fiction story, where aliens effect the transformation. Through a clever use of a new concept, McCaffrey keeps her reader's interest.

Hunger

Like other woman writers, such as Elizabeth Fischer or Laura Esquival, McCaffrey makes much of food in *Restoree*. The emphasis on food draws on traditional associations of women and cooking, women and nurturance, women and domesticity. McCaffrey's interest in food is also revealed in her two collections of recipes by science fiction writers: *Out of the World*, and a forthcoming volume. While other contemporary women writers focus on food, McCaffrey's insertion of hunger into *Restoree* is a change for science fiction. Science fiction's traditionally male heroes never think about food, and scarcely seem to eat. But McCaffrey's restoree is a very believable human being, who as she experiences exotic adventures, still feels hungry and worries about other people's eating as well. This very practical emphasis makes *Restoree*'s unbelievable adventures seem more real.

McCaffrey uses hunger to remind us that Sara is a living, breathing human being. Her repeated references to Sara's hunger and to food anchor the reader in human experience. Hunger also reminds us that Sara has been deprived—of a supportive family on Earth, of any close friends or a lover on Earth—and that on Lothar she is in danger of being executed for being a restoree. Her hunger reminds us that, even in her new, beautiful body, Sara has basic human needs. Her hunger reflects a healthy biological adaptation to her new body, and a response to others. For example, the morning after Harlan marries her, Sara wakes up tremendously hungry. This reaction echoes that of other heroines such as Scarlett O'Hara in *Gone With the Wind* the morning after Rhett, her husband, carries her up the staircase to bed. Sara can believe that Maxil, a young man, is a true friend when he sees that her hunger is satisfied with snacks and lunch. In yet another example, Sara makes sure that everyone has dinner even after an attempted rebellion in which she and her friends are threatened. Here, she fulfills a traditional female role of caretaking, but in seeing to dinner she also satisfies her own rapacious hunger. Eating creates a bond between people, as for example, when Sara, her husband Harlan, and his brother share a quiet breakfast together. Sara's hunger provides the concluding note of humor and bonding at the very end of the novel. Harlan announces his hunger, creating a parallel with her needs, and Sara laughs, "dispelling the last shadows of [her] weeks of fearful doubts and uncertainties" (252). McCaffrey uses hunger to show the humanity of her characters and to create connections between characters. Hunger functions as a refrain, and finally, as a source of humor.

A New Technology

In the same way that McCaffrey pioneers an emphasis on food and hunger with a female protagonist, so too her use of gems as technology prefigures a major trend in women's science fiction: the use of alternative, feminized technology. Not only are gems and crystals associated more with women as adornments, but their shape also represents a move away from an emphasis on explicitly masculine, phallic weaponry and ships. The term "phallic" refers to an object shaped generally like male genitalia. The weapons used by Flash Gordon and other 1940s and 1950s space heroes were invariably phallic in shape, as were their space ships. McCaffrey's switch to an alternative, gem-based technology suggests what human society may be overlooking by focusing so exclusively on the idea of weapons that are penetrating and missile-based.

The use of crystals as weapons again suggests an important change from the phallic weaponry of most science fiction space opera. To defeat the Mil, who delight in eating sentient beings after skinning them alive, Harlan, Sara's patient and lover, turns to a new innovative technology—crystals. The use of crystals (well before New Age investment in crystals as powerful) evokes witches and other feminine sources of power (see Chapter 2). The Lotharians' alternative weaponry is reflected in their treatment of women; Lothar is far ahead of Earth in its treatment of females. Although the society has a quasi-feudal structure, women are respected on Lothar, allowed to choose their own sexual partners, and to have children with a number of fathers. Sara finds this system bewildering, but after her oppression by her father and brothers she finds it quite welcome. Lothar makes Earth look backward and regressive through its openness to the feminine. McCaffrey makes her endorsement of the Lotharians explicit when the crystals provide the decisive factor in the war against the Mil.

Humor

Any discussion of *Restoree* must address the issue of tone and how it affects the reader. McCaffrey describes the novel as a " 'tongue-in-cheek protest, utilizing as many of the standard 'thud and blunder' clichés as possible with one new twist—the heroine was the viewpoint character and *she* was always Johanna-on-the-spot' " (quoted in Brizzi 13). Characterizing the book as a "parody" "to critics who took the book seriously she says, 'You *clownheads* . . . I'm teasing you!' " (quoted in Brizzi, *Anne McCaffrey* 13). Brizzi thinks that the humor may require a reader well versed in science fiction or gothic, or may simply be too subtle for most readers. However, the extreme incongruity of being skinned alive certainly suggests humor through exaggeration, as do Sara's inevitable abilities to save the day, such as when she and Harlan hide on a boat, and she, not Harlan, knows how to sail very well. There is a camp flair to the text, as when the conclusion reveals that Sara is from Earth, and a Lotharian expresses the hope that Earth is "A planet, full, I hope, of other enticing females" (245). Of course, Sara in her natural state was anything but enticing.

McCaffrey uses humor throughout her novels, and as she explains elsewhere, "one of my personal complaints of science fiction: it takes itself much too seriously" (*Alchemy and Academe* xi). After *Restoree*, and perhaps in part because of its confused reception, McCaffrey employs humor throughout her books, but she doesn't base any one text entirely on humor. As she says, humor "is one of the hardest things to carry off in a story or novel and especially in science fiction. But there are many humorous incidents in every life, so I've included such episodes in all my books" (*Get Off the Unicorn* 153).

CHARACTER DEVELOPMENT

A Woman's Rebellion

Rather remarkable for 1967, the year *Restoree* was published, Sara has clear feminist inclinations. She realizes that she is oppressed by her family, especially her brothers. When she leaves her family, Sara declares, "If I cook another meal for anyone, it'll be for myself and not for six field-hand appetites that don't know decent food from pigs' swill" (13). She continues insisting that she will not do her brothers' domestic work: "If I iron anything, it'll be my own clothing, not shirts and shirts and shirts" (14). Her father begrudges Sara her education, so she has had "to work constantly to support" (14) herself. Perplexed by her resistance to domestic drudgery and servitude, her mother insists, "The girl's ill" (14). But the reader realizes that Sara is not ill, simply properly rebelling against her family's oppression.

Sara needs her mental strength when she faces not only the ordeal and physical torture of being skinned alive and then "restored" with new skin and facial features, but also the psychologically stressful adaptation to a new world and society. In part because she had so little to live for, her adjustment to new circumstances works smoothly. Imprisoned in an asylum and forced to be an attendant to a man kept under sedation, Sara figures out how to help her "patient," arranges their escape, and facilitates their flight because she knows how to sail a ship. Sara also has another trait that enables her survival in these circumstances—she is very curious. Brizzi describes Sara as "emblematic of a feminist self-assertion *not* to be a helpless, hapless, stereotyped excuse for a character" (*Anne McCaffrey* 13). Transformed into a beauty on a world where women are free to have a variety of sexual partners, Sara must grapple with what it means to have a new kind of power. She has trouble adapting to the freedom that Lotharian women have, but she likes it. Because this novel is told in first person, from Sara's perspective, readers identify with her. They further identify with her because she is from Earth, like McCaffrey's readers. McCaffrey thus lures the readers into appreciating and admiring Sara's strength and character. In 1967, there were very few female protagonists in science fiction; Sara is remarkable not only as a precursor of McCaffrey's other strong female heroines, but also as a role model for other women science fiction writers.

How Sara Changes

The notion of a restoree, a person restored after being almost eaten by the alien abductors, is a new and original science fiction idea. The restoree concept enables McCaffrey to explore what appearance means, especially for women. Sara has been considered unattractive because of her prominent nose. Her new self, by contrast, is regarded as highly desirable. Restorees are considered abominations on Lothar, the planet on which Sara finds herself, so that while Sara enjoys prestige and attention, she must keep her restoration secret. Rescued by a Lotharian scientist from the fate of being eaten, she then becomes part of his secret and illegal experiment to restore people who have been so damaged. Apparently, no restoree had ever regained its senses, as Sara has—attributable perhaps to her Earth origins, but more likely to her strength of character. Sara's new looks are "all my most glowing dreams had once evoked" (15). But to reach this apex, Sara has had to be skinned alive, almost eaten by another alien species, the Mil, and then restored— a process extrapolated from plastic surgery, which involves pain and mutilation. Through Sara's transformation, McCaffrey comments on the distortions that women endure to reach an impossible ideal of feminine beauty. That Sara's transformation happens on another planet allows McCaffrey to suggest "not on Earth" will a woman ever become the vision of her dreams. *Restoree*'s story suggests what otherworldly or extraordinary means women go through to be considered desirable, here on Earth. Through defamiliarization (see Chapter 2), McCaffrey makes the familiar (women's beauty rituals and cosmetic surgery) seem bizarre and distorted.

THEMES

The Importance of Cooperation

Not only is the Earth backward in its treatment of women, but also in its politics. While Earth exists in isolation, the Lotharians have already cooperated with not one, but two other alien species in their attempt to defeat the Mil. As she does in her later novels, McCaffrey emphasizes the importance of cooperating with others. It is through one of the aliens that the Lotharians find the crystals that they use to defeat the Mil. If the Lotharians had allowed their terrible exploitation by the carnivorous Mil to prejudice them against other aliens, the Lotharians would never have found the weapon needed to defeat the evil Mil. Similarly, Sara must overlook Harlan's deficiencies when she first meets him. Although he is drugged and ugly to her eyes, she tries to help him. As the drugs wear off, she sees the "real" Harlan, a man who helps her in turn and with whom she falls in love. Harlan, too, must overcome prejudice against restorees. They are considered abominations who should be killed. But Harlan sees beyond Sara's origins, and is rewarded when she enables him to escape. They need each other to escape their imprisonment in a sanatorium. Harlan knows Lothar and its culture, and he can protect Sara. But he, in turn, needs Sara's sailing abilities to escape on a ship. Through Harlan and Sara's relationship and the war against the Mil, McCaffrey shows her readers the importance of cooperating with others. More specifically, she emphasizes the importance of men and women working together.

The Body

Restoree deals with the importance of the body to human beings. While the body is often taken for granted, McCaffrey stresses its constructedness. Human bodies can be changed and altered, if not yet to the degree that Sara's body is changed. But Sara's transformation is an example of defamiliarization of the human body. Her restoration evokes cosmetic surgery and cosmetics in general. How and why do humans alter their bodies? With Harlan's body, McCaffrey introduces the alteration of the body through drugs. Rather than taking a position against bodily alterations, McCaffrey asks her readers to think about such operations. Sara seems much happier in her new body, but that is mostly because she is treated better by other people. Her essential character is unchanged. Harlan, on the other hand, is affected for the worse by his unwilling drugged state. Drugs, which affect a human's personality, are presented as far more dangerous and disabling than a physical change, even a complete change like the one Sara experiences. Through this contrast McCaffrey points to an essential part of a being, the self. External appearance is presented as inessential, suggesting that we humans, and perhaps especially women, are socialized to pay too much attention to appearance.

Restoree also raises the science fiction question, "What if . . . " What if humans could completely alter their bodies? What if our obsession with physical beauty continues? What is the most important or essential part of a human being? While some science fiction presents us with unrealistic bodies (such as *Star Trek's* Captain Kirk's physique, undamaged after many fights), McCaffrey presents characters who have vulnerable, mutable bodies. This characterization reminds her readers that we have bodies too, which, like Sara and Harlan's bodies, affect our possibilities and our self-esteem.

ALTERNATE READING: FEMINIST CRITICISM

Feminism is a social movement for the social, political, and economic equality of women with men; one aspect of feminist literary criticism attempts to reach equality by focusing on female writers and characters. Feminist literary criticism is a rich and diverse field with a long history. However, this literary movement emerged with particular strength in the late 1960s and early 1970s, just as McCaffrey was becoming a bestselling author. A feminist critic stresses that gender, one's identity as either male or female, is one of the most important defining qualities of a human life; whether people are male or female affects every aspect of their existence. The issues of feminist literary criticism and feminism in general appear throughout McCaffrey's novels. Some feminist literary critics focus on female characters, or on sexism; McCaffrey's *Restoree* explores both.

As a female writer, McCaffrey invites a feminist analysis. A feminist critic would want to know how McCaffrey's experiences as a woman affect her writing. She describes her mother as a brave and versatile woman, and asks, "Is it any wonder I write about strong women?" ("Retrospection" *Women of Vision* 22). Not surprisingly, all of McCaffrey's heroines are extraordinary. Even though some of her heroines, like Sara, face seemingly impossible situations, they inevitably triumph over their sexist society. McCaffrey's female characters also face adversity, as McCaffrey herself did. She coped with her husband's hostility to her writing and she has described herself as being "psychologically battered" (E-mail 3-9-95). Nevertheless, McCaffrey persisted in her writing and triumphed over his criticism. Similarly, McCaffrey succeeded in the primarily male-dominated world of science fiction. She was the first woman to win the Hugo Award, awarded annually by the World Science Fiction Convention, and the first woman to win the Nebula, awarded by

the Science Fiction Writers of America. Her achievements make Mc-
Caffrey a role model for other women writers, and for her readers as
well.

While some feminist critics look to the gender of the writer and make
her the focus of their analysis, other feminist critics look to female characters. Again McCaffrey's work provides paradigmatic instances. Most
of McCaffrey's protagonists are, like Sara, female. In this regard alone,
McCaffrey is part of a feminist movement within science fiction. The shift
to female protagonists and to issues of concern to women, such as relationships rather than science alone, became widespread in the 1970s,
so McCaffrey here, too, was a leader of change. In this regard, science
fiction, like other literatures, reflects the society in which it is produced.
The effect of the women's movement can be seen in McCaffrey's novels.
At the same time, McCaffrey should be credited with helping make
changes in our society by creating powerful heroines with whom female
readers can identify. McCaffrey's heroines, like Sara, do not start out
powerful, but end up so by the end of the novels. Through hard work,
luck, and talent, Sara escapes imprisonment in an asylum and finds a
new and satisfying life for herself. Sara serves as a believable and realistic
role model.

McCaffrey emphasizes that her heroines are intended to be believable
characters rather than fairy tale characters. Sara might seem like a fairy
tale figure with her new beautiful body and wonderful royal lover, but
Sara's life is not idealized. Brizzi describes McCaffrey's heroines as Cin-
derellas, a description that offends McCaffrey. It might seem that with
her new skin as a parallel to Cinderella's new outfit, *Restoree* is a kind
of science fiction Cinderella. But *Restoree* is far more complicated than
the fairy tale heroine. McCaffrey writes, "My heroines are victims who
show that they can survive whatever has victimized them. This is an
important difference [from the Cinderella story] in both viewpoint and
conclusion" (E-mail 3-9-95). McCaffrey's revision of the Cinderella plot
is feminist in that it empowers the Cinderella figure.

While Sara functions as a role model, she also works to shift the emphasis in science fiction away from male characters and traditionally
masculine concerns (see Chapter 2). When male and female readers get
caught up in *Restoree* they identify with a feminine viewpoint. This shift
in perspective enables the male reader to leave his gender behind, temporarily. Only through fiction can humans experiment so widely with
point of view, for we can also see not only the alien world but also Earth
from a feminist perspective. Earth was a terrible place for Sara because

of her sexist family. Unappreciated and overworked, Sara is exploited by her male-dominated family. Sexism is also exposed in the way that Sara is judged by her appearance. The full and exciting life that Sara leads on Lothar reveals that even an unprepossessing librarian has the potential for leadership and adventure. That kind of excitement isn't available to Sara on Earth. When we enter the world of *Restoree*, we see the limitations of our own culture, especially its unfair treatment of women.

The Doona Series

Like *Restoree*, *Decision at Doona* (1969), the first volume in *The Doona* series, evokes pulp science fiction tradition, the magazines that were popular in the 1940s and 1950s and featured action-adventure tales situated in outer space. Focusing primarily on male heroes and their conflicts with aliens, these tales were read by the generation of science fiction writers who began writing in the late 1940s and early 1950s. *Decision at Doona* was written shortly after *Restoree*, so similarities in the two texts should not be surprising. *The Doona* series differs from the rest of McCaffrey's series in its use of a male hero; *Decision at Doona* focuses on a young boy, Todd, whose open-mindedness to alien contact saves humanity and the aliens from an intergalactic war. As a result of Todd's imitation of and alliance with huge cat-like creatures, he interprets for them during a conference on the planet Doona that both species claim for colonization. As Todd grows up in the subsequent novels in the series, his special role as contact with the cat people remains a focus of the series. McCaffrey continues the series with *Crisis on Doona* in 1992 and *Treaty at Doona* in 1994, both co-authored with Jody Lynn Nye. *The Doona* series thus represents both early and recent work by McCaffrey.

PLOT DEVELOPMENT

As Mary Brizzi notes, *Decision at Doona*, the first novel in *The Doona* series, "shares the premise of first-contact with *Restoree*" (Brizzi, *Anne McCaffrey* 15). But the series as a whole also shares other qualities with *Restoree*. Although *The Doona* series lacks the strong female protagonist of *Restoree*, both series emphasize the importance of cooperation between species. *Restoree* includes alternative technology through crystals, and *The Doona* series presents an alternative technology in having a teleportation grid rather than a spaceship by which the aliens move through space.

While *Restoree* deals with friendly humanoid aliens, *The Doona* series focuses on cat-like aliens. The feline aliens, or Hrrubans as they call themselves, have a well-developed culture, but it is through a child, Todd Reeve, that a successful first contact is made. Todd and his Hrubban friend, Hrriss, have a friendship that several times prevents a space war between their peoples. This unique friendship is so strong that it parallels the relationship between Sara and her alien lover in *Restoree*. In both situations, McCaffrey uses a relationship between two individuals to mirror the cooperation that species should have. The other novels in the series, *Crisis on Doona* and *Treaty at Doona*, follow the plot of the first novel so closely that only the introduction of a third alien species saves the series from being repetitive.

Decision at Doona

Decision at Doona follows *Restoree* by only two years, and thus represents, still, the early work of McCaffrey. This novel more closely resembles traditional science fiction characters and plots. The preeminence of a young, headstrong male child connects the book with many other similar fictions, from novels by Robert Heinlein such as *Have Spacesuit—Will Travel* and *Rocket Ship Galileo* to *Star Trek: The Next Generation's* Wesley Crusher. In *Decision at Doona*, humans have developed a policy of noncohabitation because of their disastrous first contact with an alien species who committed mass suicide when they met humans. This event explains the humans' insistence on a version of *Star Trek's* famous Prime Directive—noninterference with other cultures. The suicide may also evoke the environmental concerns of the 1960s in which humans began to feel ashamed of exterminating species on Earth. Desperate for more planets to colonize because of the overpopulation of the Earth, a small group of humans lands on Doona. Only after months of residence on Doona do they discover an alien cat-like species who similarly hope to colonize the planet, which they call Rrala. Todd Reeve, the six-year-old son of one of the human colonists, bonds with the Hrrubans, as the aliens call themselves, and even sports a rope tale to imitate their natural ones. He learns to speak Hrruban, and eventually ends up negotiating the treaty that calls for humans and Hrrubans to live on Doona together.

The Earth bureaucrats represent the failure of government and the importance of settlers. The survey team sent by Earth had not discovered the Hrrubans' presence or the indigenous and highly dangerous snakes. Ironically, the snakes provide the occasion for human and Hrruban co-operation. As the snakes threaten the human settlement, Todd's father sends the Hrrubans a message, asking for assistance. They return with Todd, setting the stage for negotiations. A dangerous confrontation with the snakes thus provides a crisis that moves the plot to its conclusion.

McCaffrey describes *Decision at Doona* as her only novel written about a historical event, the Vietnam War. As she says, "I have had only ONE message, flat out—and that was *Decision at Doona* which was written up as the Vietnam War hotted up" (E-mail, 3-14-95). She wrote it to protest the Vietnam War and to remind readers that "mankind will be truly mature when it no longer feels the need to force its value judgements on anyone or anything else" (E-mail 3-14-95). Physically separated by a river, the Hrrubans and humans build a bridge that symbolizes their determination to live and work together despite cultural differences. They must resist bureaucrats and soldiers from both species who are determined to break down this interspecies cooperation. Like Ursula K. Le Guin's later Vietnam novel, *The Word for World is Forest* (1972), McCaffrey's earlier text defamiliarizes Vietnam by enabling readers to explore the issues the war raised on an alien planet. The humans and Hrrubans represent two different societies—capitalist and communist, Western and Eastern, who must learn to cooperate or else suffer a bloody war that will destroy Doona and possibly their societies. McCaffrey's characters learn to accept difference and cooperate, and thus avert a war.

Crisis on Doona

Published 23 years after *Decision at Doona*, and co-authored by Jody Lynn Nye, *Crisis on Doona* closely follows some aspects of plot of the first novel. Todd and Hrriss, Todd's devoted Hrruban friend, are on a routine mission in a small spacecraft when they are led by a false distress signal to break the treaty negotiated almost 25 years earlier. As they were as children in *Decision at Doona*, Todd and Hrriss are in the center of treaty negotiations. Hunting snakes and killing Great Big Momma snakes that have gone rogue and threaten the settlements, has become a tourist attraction. The Doonans have cleverly taken what was a danger to their colony and made it a lucrative adventure. Humans and Hrrubans vacation on Doona and participate in the Hunt. After this year's Hunt, however, Todd and Hriss are imprisoned because contraband jewels have been found on their ship. The jewels had been planted by humans who wanted the treaty to be abandoned. Eventually, however, the pair are freed and vindicated, and they use their influence to have the original treaty extended. The novel focuses closely on Todd and Hrriss's homosocial bonding, on the importance of environmentalism, and on cooperation between species.

Todd and Hrriss are remarkably close, and their homosocial bonding symbolizes the closeness of the humans and Hrrubans. The pair "are much admired on Earth. Their friendship is legendary. I think that you could say that it epitomizes Doona in many people's minds" (127) explains an Earthwoman. Framing Todd and Hrriss for a crime they did not commit is a way for the prejudiced humans who hate aliens to derail the treaty renegotiations. Although by the end of the novel, both have female mates, much is made of the extraordinary nature of their relationship. Their family and friends admire their closeness, which symbolizes the possibility for human-alien relationships. "Their rapport was instinctive: they seemed to read each other's mind" (29). Even Todd's soon-to-be wife thinks, "It was nearly impossible to think of one without the other, they were so inseparable" (41–42). When Hrriss and Todd are separated to await trial for the possession of contraband material, Hrriss complains to his mother in terms that evoke a closer relationship than mere friendship, "It is so difficult to have a lifelong companion torn away from one's side, Mother" (113), and he does not want "a life without Todd in it every day" (115). Hriss's complaints and the comments of other characters make quite noticeable that a same-sex friendship can cross species lines. McCaffrey thus suggests that male bonding is more important than intra-species bonding: Gender transcends racial difference. Todd and Hriss's relationship connects with the parallel to the Vietnam War: Species difference can be seen as a metaphor for racial difference. Just as Todd and Hriss overcome prejudice, so can and should Westerners (Americans) and Easterners (North Vietnamese). McCaffrey and Nye depict Todd and Hriss's relationship as laudatory in every way.

It is unusual for McCaffrey to focus exclusively on male characters, but they can be read as coded characters. As with the identification of women viewers with Spock in the original *Star Trek*, McCaffrey's female readers can identify with Hriss. Because he cares so much for the human male, Hriss thus stands in for human females. Feline and thus symbolically associated with the feminine, Hriss represents the role that many women wish they could have: that of an equal partner with an attractive human male. In her creation of the Hrrubans, McCaffrey anticipates the use of feline aliens by other feminist science fiction writers such as C. J. Cherryh.

Treaty at Doona

Treaty at Doona complicates the conflict between two species by introducing a third, the Gringg. A huge space-faring species with tremendously advanced technology, the Gringg arrive at Doona, worrying and perplexing the governments of Hrruba and Earth who have enough difficulty dealing with each other. The colonists (the human and Hrruban settlers of Doona), by contrast, extend their spirit of interspecies cooperation to the Gringg. While Todd and Hriss are still the primary focus of the plot, the Gringg's sex roles raise the issue of gender for all three species. Each species treats sex differently, the Gringg having complete sex role reversals from the traditional male-dominated societies of humans and Hrrubans. And in a return to the spirit of the first novel, children—human, Hrruban, and Gringg—prove to be important facilitators for interspecies communication. The Gringg artistic emphasis reflects art itself as a means of breaking down cultural barriers.

All three novels follow a similar plot: a crisis, conflict with alien species about how to resolve the conflict, and resolution. *Decision at Doona* begins with a crisis of overpopulation. Humans have taxed the resources of the Earth and must desperately search for other planets to colonize. This situation is still quite possible, and it seemed especially urgent in 1969 when McCaffrey wrote this first novel in the series. Ecological concerns are the way that McCaffrey draws the reader into the events of the first book. Because human contact with another alien species resulted in the aliens' mass suicide, humans are quite leery of contact with aliens. When the human settlers of Doona discover an alien race, they are unwilling to give up the planet, but are also worried about contact with an alien species. Following how this dilemma can be resolved keeps the reader turning the pages of *Decision at Doona*. *Crisis on Doona*, as its title suggests, revisits the planet 25 years after the first treaty on Doona. The treaty is about to expire, and the crisis focuses on threats to the treaty's renewal and the possibility of a war. While the plot recreates the same elements of the drama in the first book, readers also turn to this book to find out what has happened to their favorite characters. Since twenty-five years have passed, Todd and his alien friend Hriss are now adults, but they are still close friends and still critical to resolving the crisis. *Treaty at Doona* complicates the human-Hrruban dyad by introducing a third species that seems to threaten both human and Hrruban. Should Doona's settlers attack this new alien, or will the Gringg turn out to be valuable allies? The first contact plot (see Chapter 2) keeps the reader's attention riveted to the novel. While most first contact stories involve humans and an alien species, McCaffrey complicates the simplicity of first contact by creating a triad of species. This rather direct and dramatic plot is made engaging through McCaffrey and Nye's use of characterization.

CHARACTER DEVELOPMENT

All three novels present the reader with characters whose energy and naivete make them admirable ambassadors to other species. While some science fiction stories deal cloyingly and unbelievably with children who are super heroes (such as Wesley on *Star Trek: The Next Generation*), *The Doona* series depicts children as mischievous, annoying, but ultimately very useful members of their species. There may even be an element of autobiographical knowledge here—one of McCaffrey's children is named Todd, like the human hero in the series. Todd is a likeable character, energetic and too much for his parents to handle. His exuberance and desire to explore lead him across a river and to the alien Hrubbans. Because he is young, Todd lacks the prejudice and competition with the aliens that many of the adult humans manifest. Todd adopts, and in turn is adopted by, the Hrrubans. His willingness to learn their language demonstrates how completely he identifies with them. Todd's qualities present a model for readers who may be seeking how to handle difference.

McCaffrey praises Todd's qualities of openness and acceptance and he retains these qualities into adulthood. Todd and Hriss, his Hrubban friend, remain close and fly space missions together. But in *Crisis on Doona* these two characters must also learn to mature and accept adult responsibilities. They both worry that they will lose their camaraderie if they choose female mates and raise children. Over the course of the novel, they are forcibly separated when they are charged with smuggling, and this isolation gives them a chance to realize that even distance will not dim their affection for each other. By the end of the novel each has chosen (or more accurately been chosen by) a female of their species, and they decide to settle down to the responsibility of a family. This character development reassuringly depicts this process as pleasurable. Todd and Hriss will have a different kind of relationship after they marry their female companions, but they have wisely found mates who understand and approve of their friendship.

Treaty at Doona suggests that species, too, must go through a cycle of development, and that just as Todd and Hriss must cut back on their exploring and devote more time to relationships, so too must humans and Hrrubans reach out to the Gringg. Entire species also can be seen as having character, and thus go through character development. The human and Hrruban cooperation shows that each species has changed. The humans have learned to be more careful and tolerant of difference. Similarly, the Hrrubans must learn to trust and respect human ideas. In both the individual and species, development is signalled by maturity and a respect and interest in others.

THEMES

Environmentalism

While the first novel certainly makes clear the problems caused by overpopulation of the Earth and the abuse of resources, *Crisis on Doona* is explicitly an environmental novel. One of the reasons that Doona is so special to both species is its pastoral, unspoiled state. The colonists of both species are determined to keep Doona pristine. The human and Hrruban colonists begin to see themselves not as emigrants from other planets, but as native "Doonans." "Waste, pollution, and senseless destruction of resources were avoided" (26). Doona also exemplifies environmental reclamation; horses are bred there, rescuing the species from near extinction on Earth. Because they live so naturally, Doonans are not caught up or mesmerized by forms of wealth. "It was difficult for young Doonans to take the awe and greed over such trinkets [the gems Todd and Hriss are accused of stealing] seriously" (31). Even the Snake Hunt is motivated only by the need to kill snakes who have gone rogue, threatening humans and Hrrubans alike. "The Hunt was against killing any wildlife that hadn't gone rogue. Once one had gone berserk, the Doonans had no choice" (46). This environmental consciousness connects to their pacifism; they value each other's lives, too—"there is no standing force of any kind on Doona" (93) because there is no need. McCaffrey and Nye present this respect for the natural world as an ideal that other humans should try to emulate, both in the novel and in the real world.

Cooperation

The cooperation that the human and Hrruban colonists manifest also provides an example to McCaffrey's readers. If we think back to McCaffrey's message about the Vietnam War, Doona can also represent the idea that no one group or nation should try to dominate plots of Earth. If humans and aliens can cooperate, then surely different groups of humans can. Here McCaffrey repeats a message that appears in all her fictions—the importance of overlooking cultural difference and of diverse groups working together. This message appears even more explicitly in *Treaty at Doona*, in which humans and Hrrubans encounter a third alien species.

Children and Acceptance of Difference

While a young Todd Reeve facilitates communication between alien species in *Decision at Doona*, in *Treaty at Doona* it is a group of children and a young Gringg, the child of the alien spaceship's captain, who bring the species together. The Gringg child makes the first contact with the humans and Hrrubans who enter the Gringg ship. A meter tall, he curiously sniffs Todd's father, Ken, and sneezes, even nudging him and pawing at Ken's space helmet in a clearly nonthreatening, exploratory approach. The Gringg are bulky creatures, and the females nearly 2½ meters tall with fur everywhere except their faces and forepads. With honey-colored hair, long claws, and black leathery noses, they look like huge bears. However, they have thick tails and the ability to talk. Later, when the Gringg leave their ship to visit Doona, it is Doonan children who welcome the aliens, and the children play with the Gringg child. McCaffrey and Nye endorse the unquestioning acceptance of difference by children and suggest that the adults of all three species have much to learn from their children's ready acceptance of one another. "The children had none of their parents' reserve" (87), and entrusting their children to each other's care is one way that the species can demonstrate their trust of each other. As one of the Hrrubans argues as they negotiate, "If my children and their offspring trust them, can I do less? Children are most intuitive" (274). Looking toward and emulating children's easy acceptance of difference provides a way to ease cultural difference. McCaffrey and Nye's emphasis on children also reminds us that prejudice has to be learned, that it is not innate or natural to human beings.

Gender Roles

The gender role reversals presented by the Gringg cause the humans, Hrrubans, and McCaffrey and Nye's readers to question gender stereotypes. The Gringg want to know the sex of humans before they even begin talking to them, but they mis-identify human sex characteristics. In contrast to the human and Hrruban sexual characteristics, in Gringg society females are larger than males and occupy positions of power, such as the ship's captain. When the Gringg first meet humans, they assume that Ken, Todd's father, is female because he is the tallest and because he is wearing a spacesuit that hides his genitalia. Bringing their gender stereotypes to bear causes much confusion for each species. At first, the Gringg even assume that humans and Hrrubans are the same species, female and male. Here McCaffrey and Nye draw on the long-standing science fiction tradition, discussed in Chapter 2, of depicting male and female as two different species. The comic confusion stresses the arbitrariness of gender divisions, because each species assumes its roles are "natural." For example, the Gringg captain complains that the humans' "shrill" voices hurt her ears—shrill being a stereotypical description of women's voices (53). And female Gringg are especially adept at engineering and male Gringg at the arts, an exact role reversal of human gender roles. But humans have much to learn from the Gringg, who travel with their children on exploration missions, and from the Hrrubans, who have no experience with rape; they respect their females' choices. As the Gringg captain notes, "So we have a female linguist [mis-identifying Ken] . . . we shall have to converse much on the divisions of labor among gender" (48). The necessity of conversing about gender divisions applies to humans as well as Gringg. Through the Gringg,

McCaffrey and Nye use an alien perspective to examine the arbitrary nature of human gender roles.

The Importance of Art

The Gringg's emphasis on art provides a common ground, as does the language of science, for interspecies communication. Even Ken recognizes that Gringg writing is itself a work of art (53), and the Gringg wear beautifully decorated collars. The first form of communication between the Gringg and the other two species is drawing, and the Gringg captain tells her assistant that this first contact will make a great epic poem. This captain also sings to a small child, breaking up an anxious crowd. McCaffrey and Nye draw on a pattern that runs through all of McCaffrey's fictions, from *The Brain Ship* series to *The Crystal Singer* series. McCaffrey and Nye posit art and science as universal codes that testify to the worth, as well as the sentience of beings. After first contact with the humans and Hrrubans, the Gringg begin writing, creating what Ken immediately recognizes as works of art. Their artistic nature provides one clue to their civilization, and the art also belies the evidence of a videotape, held by the Earth government, that suggests that the Gringg may be xenocides, mass murderers of other species. The high standard of Gringg art and music causes a high-ranking Hrruban to declare in the Gringg's defense: "They may have much to offer us—not only trade goods, but cultural gifts" (143). Humans also use art to communicate with the Gringg; they tell them the stories of the Three Bears and Winnie-the-Pooh, to explain how the Gringgs' bear-like appearance affects humans.

As befits a science fiction novel, however, both art and science are needed for effective communication between species. As the humans, Hrrubans, and Gringg discover when they use technology to create a translator, "the language of engineering [has] intrinsic universality" (133). Drawing on art and science enables the Gringg to make a successful trade and political exchange with the humans and Hrrubans. The Hrrubans admire the Gringg advanced music and art, and science provides the means (a translator) for humans, Hrrubans, and Gringg to communicate their needs and desires. Doona, or Doonarrala, the combination of human and Hrruban names that the colonists adopt in this novel, has become a perfect, neutral meeting place for these three species. The book concludes with the Gringg directing a fourth, newly discovered species to Doonarrala, there to learn the lessons of interspecies cooperation and the acceptance of cultural difference that the planet now exemplifies.

ALTERNATE READING: PSYCHOANALYTIC CRITICISM

Psychoanalytic criticism explores the parallels between the unconscious and fiction. Like dreams, a particular manifestation of the unconscious mind, fiction contains truth and ideas that are neither obvious nor self-evident. Both dreams and fiction must be interpreted. Drawing upon the writings of Sigmund Freud, critics have applied the discipline of psychology to fiction writing. In *The Interpretation of Dreams*, Freud describes concepts he uses to analyze dreams, and these concepts can also be used by literary critics. First, Freud identifies the idea of the unconscious, a part of the mind that we are not consciously aware of. Second, Freud theorizes that the unconscious contains repressed thoughts and ideas—ideas that are either upsetting or forbidden by our society. Third, Freud posits that all humans are sexual beings, and that many of our sexual thoughts and desires are repressed and end up in our unconscious. Understanding that the unconscious contains forbidden desires can help explain otherwise inexplicable human behavior. Freud often used psychology to explain physical illness that had no clearly identifiable physical cause.

In literary analysis, one commonly used aspect of Freud's theory is the idea of the phallic symbol. A phallic symbol represents the power associated with the father or patriarch of a family; a phallic symbol thus represents masculine power in western society. One of the symbols that Freud himself identified as a phallic symbol is a snake. Snakes are very important in *The Doona* series. They are crucial to the plot of the first book as a dangerous force, and in the second and third books snake hunts are a prime tourist activity. For those who participate in these hunts (male or female) killing two snakes represents a rite of passage and a recognition of adulthood and power. Todd and Hriss's status on Doona is reflected in their positions as leaders of the annual Hunt. The huge snakes are "the stuff of campfire stories" (39) and considered "an adulthood ritual" (40). Killing two snakes means you have succeeded in this rite of passage, and as on Earth this success is toasted with intoxicating drink. The Great Momma Snakes are particularly feared. The gendering of the biggest snakes might make it seem that they are not phallic symbols, but actually the gendering supports this reading of them as phallic symbols. In order to achieve masculinity, the snake-hunter must subdue or destroy the powerful female snake, and claim its power for him or herself. A Freudian critic would see in the snake hunt the symbolic representation of every male child's need to separate himself from his mother and identify with and emulate his father. The male characters in this story especially bond over the snakes. The nephew of Todd's archenemy (an admiral opposed to the treaties) becomes Todd's great admirer after a snake hunt. Most tellingly, even the Gringg, who are a female-dominated race, become honorary men when they relish snake meat and kill snakes. A young Gringg frightens away another predator to eat snake eggs, and his mother, the Gringg captain, receives the admiration and respect of humans and Hrrubans when she kills a Great Momma Snake with her bare hands. The Gringg kill two snakes without weapons, thus achieving adult male status. Analyzing the function of the snake in the series shows the operation and use of phallic symbols.

The Powers Series

Powers That Be (1993) and *Power Lines* (1994), the first and second books in a new series McCaffrey co-authors with Elizabeth Ann Scarborough, focus on a female protagonist who discovers love and a new life form— a sentient planet. These two novels contain a twist on first contact stories—narratives that deal with what happens when humans and aliens meet each other for the first time. Yana, the protagonist of *Powers That Be* and *Power Lines,* is an older woman who discovers a new type of sentience in a planet that is itself alive. Fighting for the Petaybee, the planet, Yana forces her company to acknowledge the planet's rights.

In contrast to the compact charms of *Restoree,* this new series promises to be one of McCaffrey's expansive universes. *Powers That Be* and *Power Lines* contain the features that are central to McCaffrey's fiction: a strong female protagonist, an emphasis on environmentalism, the power of art, and the importance of tolerance. The series may be her most successful collaboration, perhaps in part because the process of creation differs from that of her other co-authored series. The other co-authored series begin with a book written by McCaffrey alone, and then the other writers develop her concept under her guidance. In *The Powers* series, McCaffrey and Scarborough created the concept together and actually worked together on the same computer disk. As McCaffrey explains, "She was in my house [visiting] so we could thrash plot elements back and forth until we had them where we wanted them" (E-mail 4-12-95). In *Powers That*

Be, Yana travels to the planet Petaybee for the first time; *Power Lines* follows her further struggles (and the planet's) to have Petaybee's sentience acknowledged and respected. A third volume in the series is forthcoming.

SERIES DEVELOPMENT

Powers That Be

Major Yanaba Maddock has been altered, not by aliens as Sara was in *Restoree*, but by a terrorist attack that has left her with debilitated lungs. Sent by her company to Petaybee (ironically named for the "powers that be"), a terraformed planet with Arctic-like conditions, Yana is asked to spy on the inhabitants in order to explain both the disappearance of exploration teams and the company's inability to locate mineral and other deposits that space surveys reveal are on Petaybee. Yana's discoveries and her restoration to health are accompanied by her falling in love with a native of the planet, and with the planet itself. In a science fiction development of the Gaia hypothesis, which asks us to look at Earth as a living, whole organism, the planet of Petaybee itself turns out to be sentient and active.

Power Lines

Power Lines also focuses on Yana, but expands our attention to three other female characters, a young female native who is exploited and abused in a religious cult on the other side of Petaybee, and Clodagh and Bunny, who appear in the first volume but who are more developed in the second book. The young native has been given the unpleasant name of "Goat Dung" (known as G-D) by the religious leader who wishes to make her one of his many wives. She escapes from the tribe, however, with the help of a wild, sentient cat, Coaxtl. Cats are very important to Clodagh, too, because although her cats are domesticated, they communicate telepathically with her, keeping her informed of all activities on the planet. The novel is even dedicated to cats: "two fur gentlemen of great dignity and courage who have meant a great deal to both of us in their separate ways and on different continents: Mr. Peaches & Simon Big-Paws." The respect for animals that characterizes much of

McCaffrey's fiction appears prominently in *Power Lines*. The cats prove instrumental in helping the planet assert its sentience and in helping the human rebels. Clodagh, Bunny, and G-D turn out to be related, and through the portrait of younger and older women rebels, McCaffrey and Scarborough point to the importance of women's autonomy and strength at all ages.

In both novels, the plot develops through one character's journey of self-discovery. In *Powers That Be*, Yana must reorient herself after her disability. She discovers new strengths of character as she decides to defend the planet rather than her employer. Her openness to difference is rewarded when she finds a lover and when her physical disabilities are healed by the planet. Similarly, *Power Lines* has the reader identify with G-D, who undergoes an equally transforming experience. Despised and abused by the tribe who has killed her parents, G-D runs away to find a new life and a new identity. Following these characters as they change and as they fight for Petaybee's status as a sentient being makes the struggle poignant and compelling.

CHARACTER DEVELOPMENT

Strong Female Protagonists

Yana represents a heroine very much like Sara from *Restoree*. Strong, courageous, and curious, Yana doesn't hesitate when she faces adventure or danger. She is described as "company soldier, investigator, explorer, training officer, and most recently, long-term resident of a medical facility" (3). Even though she is supposed to be a medical retiree, Yana finds herself recruited to do intelligence work on Petaybee. Yana resists being blackmailed to be a spy on Petaybee, and when she first steps on the planet decides to go with a female shuttle driver rather than the obnoxious male driver who tries to force her to travel with him. Her independence and support of other women continue through the novel. She bonds with Clodagh, a native who is a very large woman and powerful healer. Yana resists the efforts of the bureaucrats on Petaybee to get her to change her report on the planet. She resents the behavior and obtuseness of company officials. "After killing everyone around her [on her previous mission] and half killing her, the company still allowed brass-assed spooks like him to threaten to withhold medical treatment and to dump her unprepared in a place like this in order to use her" (100). In her purposeful resistance to corrupt company policies, Yana saves the planet from destruction and exploitation. Like Sara, Caissa [from the novel *The Coelura*], and many other McCaffrey heroines, Yana's strength of character and determination are vindicated when they save not only her life but those of many others, even an entire planet.

Yana is not the only strong female character in *The Powers* series. Clodagh has witchlike powers associating her with nature and with the planet. Even her description emphasizes the parallel: "The woman was like the planet: round, subtly active, and full of strategies" (9). Clodagh uses her understanding of nature to fight the company's attempt to control Petaybee. She communicates with her cats to find out what the company men are doing around the planet. When a sealant is used to close off part of the planet, Clodagh uses a "weed" to break up the concrete-like material in minutes. This same weed also kills the religious leader who had tried to rape Bunny.

Clodagh and the other female characters fight against male dominance and cruelty, and the mistreatment of women is connected to the abuse of the planet. Satok, a corrupt shaman, decides to ignore the planet and exploit it by assisting in the mining operations. His cruelty to Petaybee is paralleled by his cruelty to women. He abducts Bunny and attempts to rape her. In a terrifying scene, Bunny fights back and escapes. When Bunny's friend Diego arrives, he yells, "He was going to *rape* you!" and Bunny replies "He's already *raped* our planet" and she explains what Satok has done. Bunny's strength prefigures the determination and resistance that are needed to force greedy men like Satok out of power.

G-D or Cita, as her family had named her, also faces the prospect of rape by the leader of her community, known as the Shepherd. Desperate, she escapes into the wilds, where finds the wildcat Coaxtl. Cita has no faith in herself, but the cat nurtures and protects her until she can find other supportive human beings including Bunny (her sister) and Clodagh. The wise Coaxtl explains, "Home has what one needs. If we keep looking, we will find what you need here" (35). Clodagh, Bunny, and Cita all find love and solace with each other and with supportive men, suggesting that female strength and determination will be rewarded.

These female characters prompt some of the male characters to change. Diego, the son of a visiting company official, also listens to the planet, falls in love with Bunny—Petaybee's influence even clears up his acne. Dr. Whittaker Fiske, who is the scientist in charge of the planet-transforming technology that threatens Petaybee, finds Clodagh an inspiration. Through her influence, he realizes that Petaybee defies all his previous training and experience with planets. At the end of the novel, he tempers his traditional scientific beliefs and speaks in defense of the planet.

THEMES

Environmentalism

Powers That Be contains one of McCaffrey's strongest statements on environmentalism. The natives of Petaybee develop a strong symbiosis with the planet, which provides them with extraordinary endurance and other physical strengths. Yana even benefits from the planet's powers when her damaged lungs are completely restored. Just as remarkable is the planet's restoration of her reproductive powers, even though she is beyond childbearing age. The planet rejuvenates those who can appreciate and hear its message. McCaffrey and Scarborough seem to imply that if the inhabitants take care of the planet, it will take care of them. The planet's cure is, as Yana acknowledges, far in advance of technology. In fact, Yana even uses the planet's abilities to bribe the company to work with rather than against the planet. Like the rainforests, whose defenders point to the miraculous and crucial cures developed from rainforest material, Petaybee deserves to be protected from mineral harvesting and other exploitations because of what it has to offer humanity. McCaffrey and Scarborough also advocate a life lived with nature. "A healthy life in the outdoors, with untainted air to breathe and decent food to eat, was certainly providing cures never found in an Intergal [company] medical cabinet" (142). Not only is such a lifestyle on an unpolluted planet healthier, but it is also more pleasurable. Communicating with the planet is extremely gratifying—Yana describes it as ' "this *blissful* form of communication" (192). But the main environmental statement is that the planet does not belong to anybody. As one of the natives explains to Intergal officials: "The message is that Petaybee is a living sentient entity. . . . It does not wish to have its skin blown open, its flesh dug and taken away, its substance reduced, its children hunted, harvested, or remade against their will" ' (300). This powerful personification of the planet and the description of its exploitation are moving and compelling.

Similarly, *Power Lines* explores the importance of respecting plant, animal, and planet life—life in any form. McCaffrey and Scarborough use

the abuse of a life form to signify the evil of certain characters. For example, Satok, the false shaman, has all the cats in his village killed and
uses a staff with a cat's skull on it. His fear of and abuse of cats represents his inhumanity, so we are not surprised when he tries to rape
Bunny. In the same way, Matthew, a scientist for the company, orders
Coaxtl killed. In a traditionally masculine scientific ethos, he wants to
kill and study, rather than understand animals. (Fortunately, the humane
vet to whom he gives that order does not kill Coaxtl). Both Satok and
Matthew are punished—Satok is strangled by a plant, and Matthew has
his legs broken in an earthquake. Failing to respect nature has a high
cost. At the same time, respecting animal life brings great rewards. Cita
escapes from rape and a miserable existence through the help of Coaxtl,
and Clodagh receives information from cat "spies." As in *Powers That
Be*, Petaybee has remarkable restorative powers—it restores another
company scientist, Whittaker Fiske, to health and cures Diego's acne.

The Power of Art

As it does in *Restoree* and *Treaty at Doona*, art provides a means of
communication and a key to merit. In *Powers That Be*, Yana has suffered
terribly from the terrorist attack, physically and psychologically. Her
lover Sean encourages her to describe what happened to her through a
song. At first she resists, not wanting to remember the terrorist attack,
but then she composes a song about her experiences. It turns out not to
be an ordeal but a release. Singing is a form of communication and expression. As one of the natives explains to Yana, "A song has to be sung
from one person to another to be any good" (52). Songs are especially
important because few Petaybeens can read or write. They communicate
and commune with the planet by chanting songs to it. Art, then, provides
a means of communication that overcomes cultural difference, as it does
in so many of McCaffrey's fictions.

Power Lines, too, stresses the special role of music and songs. Songs
play a central part in the campaign to get all the natives to understand
the importance of respecting the planet. Diego recalls the effect of "the
old radical songs from Earth" (20). And Clodagh displays a nonjudg-
mental art aesthetic when she insists, "Each song is a good song if it
says what the singer means it to say" (21). Diego manages to make a
guitar, and he uses it to sing about the damage that has been done to
Petaybee. His music and other songs galvanize the population. The novel

concludes with the planet itself singing to the humans, "Songs we'll make, songs we'll make" (313), suggesting the collaborative nature of art.

Tolerance and Cooperation

Powers That Be emphasizes the importance of respecting cultural difference and of cooperating with others. Yana benefits tremendously as a result of her openmindedness to Petaybee and its inhabitants. She regains her health and has the opportunity to bear a child. As it does in Victorian novels, Yana's pregnancy at the end of the novel signals the start of a new life—not only literally, but also metaphorically for the planet and presumably Intergal, the company, as well. The novel implies that treating Petaybee respectfully and as an equal will bring unimaginable benefits to the company and humanity.

Similarly, Dr. Whittaker Fiske, the company scientist sent to oversee the transformation and control of Petaybee, converts to recognizing Petaybee's sentience and rights. He is rewarded with renewed vigor and a sexual relationship with Clodagh. Yana's openmindedness is also rewarded and emphasized in *Power Lines* through her sexual relationship with Sean, who is half seal. In either form, "he understood himself thoroughly and was most adept at using all of his resources to guide her into uncharted channels of pleasure" (29). Another of the company investigators, Marmiom, feels "almost effervescent. And she hadn't experienced *that* buoyancy in a long, long, time" (144). The planet proves to be valuable not only to individuals, but also to the company. As Marmion explains, "Petaybee is more important to Integral for a heretofore unexplored source of *renewable* wealth" (292). Working with the planet will be far more profitable than struggling (so far unsuccessfully) to dominate it. The planet wants to work with people rather than destroy them. At the novel's conclusion, a minister from the Collective Interplanetary Societies "speaks" with Petaybee and declares it sentient, with "boundless . . . unchartable . . . unfathomable" potential (313). This confirmation serves to underscore the message that planet and people must work together instead of fighting each other.

Like *The Powers* series, an earlier short novel, *The Coelura*, also deals with themes of environmentalism, the necessity of respecting all forms of life and the reward of love for a protagonist who demonstrates tolerance and understanding of cultural difference. Caissa, the young daughter of a minister, crashes her space car and discovers the coelura, a life form that spins beautiful rainbows that can be adapted to spectacular clothing, transforming whoever wears them. The coelura are in danger of extinction because of the human demand and greed for the fabric the creatures produce. When Caissa crashes in a coelura habitat, she also discovers a handsome young man, who is heir to property that contains the coelura, and who has vowed to protect them. Together, Caissa and Murell successfully fight to save the coelura homeland and protect them from exploitation.

Environmentalism and Art

The coelura's compassion causes it to attune itself to human needs, thus making the creatures vulnerable to human exploitation. But with Caissa and Murell's help, the coelura are protected through the creation of a preserve. The environmental message of the book is clear—natural beauty must and can be protected from human greed. Working with the coelura rather than exploiting them means more of the desirable garments will be available over a longer period of time. The coelura also deserve to be nurtured not only because of their loving natures and beauty, but also because they respond to art. As in *The Brain Ship* and *The Crystal Singer* series (see Chapter 5), art demonstrates the sentience and worth of beings. The coelura demonstrate their sentience by their interaction with Murell's music. Their response to music also provides protection, because they have learned to react only to a certain pattern of notes. Short and sweet, *The Coelura* contains McCaffrey's messages about cooperation and environmentalism. The novel prepares for McCaffrey and Scarborough's further development of similar ideas.

ALTERNATE READING: "GREEN" OR ECOFEMINIST READING

The word "Green" has been associated with many environmental movements and even a political party in Germany. Reading McCaffrey's novels through a Green prism helps us see her ecofeminist leanings. Ecofeminism is the term that describes a social and political movement that connects ecology or environmental concerns with those of feminism. The term combines the two words because ecofeminists see an integral relationship between ecological and feminist perspectives. Such critics believe that feminists must be concerned with ecology, and ecologists with feminism. Ecology is the study of organisms in relation to the environment. There are many reasons for asserting this connection, and McCaffrey supports this interpretation in the novels discussed in this chapter.

First, nature's gendering helps explain "ecofeminism." Nature has historically been identified as female. In ancient myths, a goddess has usually represented the Earth. The Earth is depicted as our mother, not only of humanity, but of all life. Much of our language about the Earth is gendered. The Earth "gives birth" to species, both plant and animal. The idea of "raping" the Earth is frequently used to describe pollution, strip-mining, and other activities that damage the planet and its ecosystem of animal and plant life. The natural world is also described as feminine. Scientists frequently use metaphors that depict science and scientists as males pursuing the reluctant mysterious female, Nature. Science fiction frequently echoes this approach, as for example in pulp science fiction stories from the 1940s and 1950s, in which male heroes fall in love with female aliens who are mermaids, lamia, or other creatures associated with the natural world. Because human society is male-dominated, we do not respect anything identified as female. Whether nature has been identified as female because we tend not to respect it, or whether nature is not respected because it has become associated with the feminine does not make a difference. The association of nature and the female, however, means that feminists and ecologists have something in common.

For many people, ecology refers to the ways in which humanity no longer functions in harmony with the Earth. In part, we have lost our respect for the Earth, this position explains, because we now rely too much on technology without considering its effects on the Earth. To recover our respect for our planet, we must simultaneously recover our respect for what is feminine.

McCaffrey's and McCaffrey and Scarborough's novels fit in well with an ecofeminist perspective. By using strong female characters, the authors present us with positive role models of femininity. Sara, Caissa, Yana, Clodagh, Bunny, and Cita all point to the ways that women can use their strength to resist sexist depictions and treatment of women. But the novels in which they appear are not simply about treating women better—they are also about treating other forms of life, especially planets, with respect. In *Restoree*, the aliens use crystals rather than damaging technology like nuclear weapons to protect themselves from attack. In

The Coelura, McCaffrey stresses that it is not only the individual coelura, but also their habitat that must be protected in order for the creatures to survive. These are important issues in the United States in 1996; the United States Supreme Court is hearing arguments about whether the Endangered Species Act can be invoked to keep lumber companies from destroying forests where the endangered spotted owl lives, and some members of Congress are suggesting a rollback of legislation that protects the environment. McCaffrey's science fiction is just as relevant today as it was a decade ago. In *Powers That Be* and *Power Lines*, McCaffrey and Scarborough make explicit connections between not just a species but an entire planet and the humans who live on it. Making Petaybee literally sentient and "alive" like humans forces us to look at planets in a new light—as beings, rather than as places. McCaffrey and Scarborough explicitly connect this ecological view to feminism. The people who are the most connected to Petaybee are women: Yana, Clodagh, and Marmion, and they use intuition and witchlike powers to communicate with the planet. The scientists must either convert to this new attitude or be punished, and those who fail to respect the planet are depicted as evil. Mistreatment of women is explicitly connected to mistreatment of the planet. *Restoree* and *The Coelura* contain elements of ecofeminism, but *The Powers* series overtly and clearly promotes an ecofeminist view. When women and planets are treated well, there will be huge benefits to society, such as the great organic, renewable wealth that Petaybee will share with humanity. An ecofeminist critic would see McCaffrey and Scarborough's series as depicting a utopian future in which ecofeminist attitudes prevail.

Bibliography

WORKS BY ANNE McCAFFREY

Alchemy and Academe. New York: Doubleday, 1970; edited by Anne McCaffrey.
All the Weyrs of Pern. New York: Ballantine, 1991.
The Chronicles of Pern: First Fall. New York: Ballantine, 1993.
The City Who Fought. New York: Baen Books, 1993; with S. M. Stirling.
The Coelura. New York: Ballantine, 1987.
Cooking Out of This World. New York: Ballantine, 1973; edited by Anne McCaffrey.
Crisis on Doona. New York: Ace, 1992; with Jody Lynn Nye.
Crystal Line. New York: Ballantine, 1992.
Crystal Singer. New York: Ballantine, 1982.
Damia. New York: Ace, 1992.
Damia's Children. New York: Ace, 1993.
The Death of Sleep. New York: Baen, 1990; with Jody Lynn Nye.
Decision at Doona. New York: Ballantine, 1969.
Dinosaur Planet. New York: Ballantine, 1978.
Dinosaur Planet Survivors. New York: Ballantine, 1984.
The Dolphins of Pern. New York: Ballantine, 1994.
Dragonsdawn. New York: Ballantine, 1988.
Dragondrums. New York: Ballantine, 1979.
Dragonflight. New York: Ballantine, 1968.
The Dragonlover's Guide to Pern. New York: Ballantine, 1989; with Jody Lynn Nye.
Dragonquest. New York: Ballantine, 1971.

Dragonsinger. New York: Ballantine, 1977.
Dragonsong. New York: Ballantine, 1976.
Generation Warriors. New York: Baen, 1991; with Elizabeth Moon.
Get Off the Unicorn. New York: Ballantine, 1977.
The Girl Who Heard Dragons. New York: Ballantine, 1994.
Killashandra. New York: Ballantine, 1985.
The Kilternan Legacy. New York: Dell, 1975.
The Lady. New York: Ballantine, 1987.
Lyon's Pride. New York: Ace, 1994.
The Mark of Merlin. New York: Dell, 1971.
Moreta: Dragonlady of Pern. New York: Ballantine, 1983.
Nerilka's Story. New York: Ballantine, 1986.
PartnerShip. New York: Baen Books, 1992; with Margaret Ball.
Pegasus in Flight. New York: Ballantine, 1990.
The People of Pern. Norfolk, Va.: Donning Co., 1988; with Robin Wood.
Power Lines. New York: Ballantine, 1994; with Elizabeth Ann Scarborough.
Powers That Be. New York: Ballantine, 1993; with Elizabeth Ann Scarborough.
The Renegades of Pern. New York: Ballantine, 1989.
Restoree. New York: Ballantine, 1967.
Ring of Fear. New York: Dell, 1971.
The Rowan. New York: Ace, 1990.
Sassinak. New York: Baen, 1990; with Elizabeth Moon.
The Ship Who Sang. New York: Ballantine, 1969.
The Ship Who Searched. New York: Baen Books, 1992; with Mercedes Lackey.
The Ship Who Won. New York: Baen, 1994; with Jody Lynn Nye.
Stitch in Snow. New York: Tor, 1984.
Treaty at Doona. New York: Ace, 1994.
To Ride Pegasus. New York: Ballantine, 1973.
The White Dragon. New York: Ballantine, 1978.
The Wings of Pegasus (*To Ride Pegasus* and *Pegasus in Flight*). Garden City: Guild
    America Books, 1991.
The Year of The Lucy. New York: Tor, 1986.

WORKS ABOUT ANNE McCAFFREY

Allen, David. *Science Fiction Readers' Guide.* Mass.: Centennial Press, 1974.
Anderson, Poul. "Starflights and Fantasies: Sagas Still to Come." In *The Craft of
    Science Fiction.* Ed. Reginald Bretnor. New York: Harper & Row, 1976. 22–
    35.
Arbur, Rosemarie. *Leigh Brackett, Marion Zimmer Bradley, Anne McCaffrey: A Pri-
    mary and Secondary Bibliography.* Boston: G. K. Hall, 1982.
Asimov, Isaac. *Asimov on Science Fiction.* Garden City, N.Y.: Doubleday, 1981.

Barr, Marleen. *Lost in Space: Probing Feminist Science Fiction and Beyond*. Chapel Hill, N.C.: University of North Carolina Press, 1993.

———. "Science Fiction and the Fact of Women's Repressed Creativity: Anne McCaffrey Portrays a Female Artist." *Extrapolation: A Journal of Science Fiction and Fantasy* 23, 1 (1982): 70–76.

Benson, Gordon H., Jr. *Anne Inez McCaffrey: Dragonlady and More*. Galactic Central Publication, 1984.

Benson, Gordon, Jr., and Phil Stephenson-Payne. "Anne McCaffrey: Dragonlady and More: A Working Bibliography." Cited in *Encyclopedia of Science Fiction*. Eds. John Clute and Peter Nicholls. New York: St. Martin's Press, 1993: 747.

Bleiler, E. F. *Science Fiction Writers: Critical Studies of the Major Authors from the Early Nineteenth Century to the Present Day*. New York: Charles Scribner's Sons, 1982.

Bretnor, Reginald. "Anne McCaffrey." *Science Fiction, Today and Tomorrow*. New York: Harper & Row, 1974: 293–294.

Brizzi, Mary T. *Anne McCaffrey*. Ed. Roger C. Schlobin. Vol. 30 in the Starmont House Reader's Guide series. Mercer Island, WA: Starmont House, 1986.

———. "Anne McCaffrey, Anne (Inez)." In *Twentieth-Century Science-Fiction Writers*. Ed. Curtis C. Smith. New York: St. Martin's Press, 1981: 364.

———. "Narcissism and Romance in Anne McCaffrey's *Restoree*; Academic Programming at Chicon IV." In *Patterns of the Fantastic*. Ed. Donald M. Hassler. Mercer Island, WA: Starmont House, 1983: 41-46.

Brown, Charles. "Nebula Awards." *Locus* 50 (1970): 1–2.

Campbell, John W. Jr. "The Place of Science Fiction." *Modern Science Fiction*. New York: Couard McCann, 1953: 4–22.

Carter, Paul A. *The Creation of Tomorrow*. New York: Columbia University Press, 1977.

Clarke, Arthur C. "Computers and Cybernetics." In *The Visual Encyclopedia of Science Fiction*. Ed. Brian Ash. New York: Harmony Books, 1977: 187–188.

Cranny-Francis, Anne. *Feminist Fictions: Feminist Uses of Generic Fiction*. New York: St. Martin's, 1990.

del Rey, Lester. "Such Stuff as Dreams." *Analog* 96, 10 (1976): 171.

Dohner, Jan. "Literature of Change: Science Fiction and Women." *Top of the News* Spring (1978): 261–265.

Donawerth, Jane. *Science Fiction by Women: Problems of Gender and Genre* (forthcoming).

Ehrenreich, Barbara and Deidre English. *Witches, Midwives, and Nurses*. Old Westbury, N.Y.: The Feminist Press, 1973.

Ellison, Harlan. "A Voice from the Styx." In *The Book of Ellison*. Ed. Andrew Porter. New York: Algol, 1978: 127–140.

Elrick, George S. *Science Fiction Handbook*. Chicago: Chicago Review Press, 1978.

Fergus, George. "A Checklist of SF Novels with Female Protagonists." *Extrapolation* 18, 1 (1976): 20–27.

Fonstad, Karen Wynn. *The Atlas of Pern*. New York: Ballantine, 1984.

Gerrold, David. "Anne McCaffrey: A Profile." *Luna Monthly* 11 (1970): 6–7, 11.

Gibson, Susan, Steven Jay Rubin, and A. J. Foster. "Secrets of the Dragonriders." *Princessions* 14 (1983): 8–21.

Gordon, Andrew. "Human, More or Less: Man-Machine Communion in Samuel R. Delany's *Nova* and Other Science Fiction Stories." In *The Mechanical God, Machines in Science Fiction*. Eds. Thomas P. Dunn and Richard D. Erlich. Westport, Conn.: Greenwood Press, 1982: 193–202.

Greenberg, Martin, and Richard Gilliam, eds. *Confederacy of the Dead*. New York: Penguin, 1993.

Gubar, Susan. "C. L. Moore and the Conventions of Women's Science Fiction." *Science Fiction Studies* 20, 7 (1980): 16–27.

Hargreaves, Matthew D. *Anne Inez McCaffrey: Two More Years of Publishing, A Bibliography of Only U.S. and U.K. Editions* (includes the complete bibliography of McCaffrey's work, including novels, short fiction, unpublished work, and plays). Seattle: Matthew D. Hargreaves, 1994.

———. *Anne Inez McCaffrey: Forty Years of Publishing, An International Bibliography*. Seattle: Matthew Hargreaves, 1992.

Harrison, M. John. "Absorbing the Miraculous." In *New Worlds #6*. New York: Avon, 1975: 221–225.

Heldreth, Lillian M. "Speculations on Heterosexual Equality: Morris, McCaffrey, Le Guin." In *Erotic Universe: Sexuality and Fantastic Literature*. Ed. Donald Palumbo. Westport, Conn.: Greenwood, 1986: 209–220.

Highland, Angela, and Cync Spear. "The Dragonlady Lands in America/Anne McCaffrey on Dragonriders, Crystal Singers and Self." *Low Orbit* 41 (1988): 31–33.

Holliday, Liz. "Reptile Romance." *Fear* 39 (1991): 20–21.

Jones, Anne Hudson. "The Cyborg (R)evolution in Science Fiction." In *The Mechanical God: Machines in Science Fiction*. Eds. Thomas P. Dunn and Richard D. Erlich. Westport, Conn.: Greenwood, 1982: 203–209.

Kagle, Steven. "Science Fiction as Simulation Game." In *Many Futures, Many Worlds*. Ed. Thomas D. Clareson. Kent, Ohio: Kent State University Press, 1977: 224–236.

Knight, Damon. "What Is Science Fiction?" In *Turning Points: Essays on the Art of Science Fiction*. Ed. Damon Knight. New York: Harper & Row, 1977: 62–69.

Landow, George P. "And the World Became Strange." In *The Aesthetics of Fantasy Literature and Art*. Ed. Roger C. Schlobin. Notre Dame, Ind.: University of Notre Dame Press, 1982: 131.

Le Guin, Ursula K. *The Language of the Night*. New York: Putnam's, 1979.

Lundwall, Sam J. "Women, Robots and Other Peculiarities." In *Science Fiction: What It's All About*. Ed. Sam J. Lundwall. New York: Ace Books, 1971: 143–179.

McCaffrey, Anne. "Retrospection." *Women of Vision*. Ed. Denise DuPont. N.Y.: St. Martin's, 1988.

Mallardi, Bill, and Bill Powers. *The Double Bill Symposium*. Akron, Ohio: D. B. Press, 1969.

Mathews, Patricia. "Dragons and Daughters." *The Stone and the Stars*, 2, 1 (March 1981): 9–11, 24.

Meyers, Walter E. *Aliens and Linguists: Language Study and Science Fiction*. Athens, Ga.: University of Georgia Press, 1980: 47.

Morgan, Chris. "Science Fiction with Dragons." *Extro* 1, 3 (1982): 18–22.

Naha, Ed. "Living with Dragons/Anne McCaffrey." *Future* 6 (1978): 22–23, 74.

Nye, Jody Lynn, with Anne McCaffrey. *The Dragonlover's Guide to Pern*. New York: Ballantine, 1989.

Palmer, Jessica. "Dragons and Beyond." *Million: The Magazine of Popular Fiction* 3 (1991): 13–17.

Panshin, Alexei, and Cory Panshin. "Science Fiction: New Trends and Old." In *Science Fiction, Today and Tomorrow*. Ed. Reginald Bretnor. New York: Harper & Row, 1975: 217–233.

Pindar, Steve. "Dragondame: An Interview with Anne McCaffrey." *Fantasy Media* 1, 2 (1979): 3–4.

Pournelle, Jerry, ed. *Nebula Award Stories*. New York: Holt, Rinehart and Winston, 1982.

Raymer, Anne Carolyn. "*The Ship Who Sang*." In *Survey of Science Fiction Literature*. Ed. Frank N. Magill. Englewood Cliffs, N.J.: Salem Press, 1979.

Roberts, Robin. *A New Species: Gender and Science in Science Fiction*. Urbana, Ill.: University of Illinois Press, 1993.

Salmonson, Jessica Amanda. "Gender Structuring of Shell Persons in *The Ship Who Sang*." *New York Review of Science Fiction* 10 (1989): 15–18.

Schmidt, Stanley. "Science in Science Fiction." In *Many Futures, Many Worlds*. Ed. Thomas D. Clareson. Kent, Ohio: Kent State University Press, 1977: 27–49.

Scholes, Robert, and Eric S. Rabkin. *Science Fiction: History, Science, Vision*. New York: Oxford University Press, 1977: 186.

Schwartz, Susan. "Women and Science Fiction." *New York Times Book Review*, 2 May 1982: 11, 26–27.

Searles, Baird, Martin Last, Beth Meacham, and Michael Franklin. *A Reader's Guide to Science Fiction*. New York: Avon, 1979: 117–118.

Slotkin, Alan R., and Robert F. Bode. "A Back (to the Future) Formation." *American Speech: A Quarterly of Linguistic Usage* 68, 3 (1993): 323–327.

Snow, C. P. *The Two Cultures: And a Second Look.* New York: Cambridge University Press, 1964.

Warrick, Patricia S. *The Cybernetic Imagination in Science Fiction.* Cambridge, Mass.: MIT Press, 1980.

Wendell, Carolyn. "The Alien Species: A Study of Women Characters in the Nebula Award Winners, 1965–1973." *Extrapolation* 20, 4 (1979): 343–354.

White, James. "Biologies and Environments." In *The Visual Encyclopedia of Science Fiction.* Ed. Brian Ash. New York: Harmony Books, 1977: 92.

Wolfe, Gary K. "The Encounter with Fantasy." In *The Aesthetics of Fantasy Literature and Art.* Ed. Roger C. Schlobin. Notre Dame, Ind.: University of Notre Dame Press, 1982: 7.

———. *The Known and the Unknown: The Iconography of Science Fiction.* Kent, Ohio: Kent State University Press, 1979.

Wolinsky, Ron and Laurence Davidson. "Rigel Interviews Anne McCaffrey." *Rigel Science Fiction* 3 (1982): 19–24.

Wood, Robin. *The People of Pern.* Norfolk, Va.: Donning Co., 1988.

Wood, Susan. "Women and Science Fiction." *Algol* 16, 1 (1978): 9–18.

Woodall, Kermit (a.k.a. Captain Video). "In Conference: Anne McCaffrey." *Low Orbit* 2, 46 (1991): 12–17.

Wytenbroek, J. R. "The Child as Creator in McCaffrey's Dragonsong and Dragonsinger." *The Lion and the Unicorn: A Critical Journal of Children's Literature* 16, 2 (1992): 210–214.

Zeek, A. E., et al. *Pern Portfolio.* Staten Island, N.Y.: Isis/Yggdrisil Press, 1978.

REVIEWS AND CRITICISM

CHAPTER 1

Alchemy and Academe

Library Journal, 15 May 1971: 1783.
Library Journal, 15 February 1971: 748.
Library Journal, 1 December 1970: 4194.
Publisher's Weekly, 12 October 1970: 50.

Cooking Out of This World

Locus, November 1992: 55.
Publisher's Weekly, 4 June 1973: 91.

Futurelove (*"The Greatest Love"*)

School Library Journal, September 1977: 153.
Library Journal, 15 June 1977: 1407.

The Lady

Inside Books, November 1988: 50.
Publisher's Weekly, 16 October 1987: 72.
Kirkus Reviews, 15 September 1987: 1343.

Stitch in Snow

Library Journal, 1 May 1985: 79.
Booklist, 15 March 1985: 1030.
Kirkus Reviews, 1 March 1985: 195.
Science Fiction Chronicle, February 1985: 4.

Three Gothic Novels (*The Kilternan Legacy, The Mark of Merlin, Ring of Fear*)

Booklist, 1 November 1990: 501.
Publisher's Weekly, 3 November 1975: 73.

The Year of the Lucy

Best Sellers, Fall 1987: 418.
Publisher's Weekly, 18 July 1986: 80.
Kirkus Reviews, 15 July 1986: 1052.
Library Journal, January 1986: 103.
Publisher's Weekly, 6 December 1985: 70.

CHAPTER 3

Dragonflight

Magpies, March 1994: 33.
Locus, October 1993: 54.
Science Fiction Chronicle, June 1993: 33.
Locus, May 1993: 51.
Locus, October 1989: 49.
School Library Journal, Spring 1988: 121.
English Journal, November 1984: 89.
English Journal, October 1980: 74.
English Journal, October 1977: 93.
Times Literary Supplement, 16 October 1969: 1215.
Publisher's Weekly, 8 July 1968: 166.

CHAPTER 4

THE DRAGONRIDERS OF PERN SERIES (DRAGONFLIGHT AND PEOPLE OF PERN dISCUSSED IN CHAPTER 3)

All the Ways of Pern

Voice of Youth Advocates, December 1993: 278.
Voice of Youth Advocates, April 1993: 9.
Kliatt Young Adult Paperback Book Guide, March 1993: 18.
School Library Journal, June 1992: 148.
Voice of Youth Advocates, April 1992: 45.
Booklist, 17 January 1992: 872.
Locus, December 1991: 54.
Library Journal, 15 November 1991: 111.
Locus, November 1991: 27.
Booklist, 1 October 1991: 202.

The Chronicles of Pern: First Fall

Analog, May 1994: 163.
Voice of Youth Advocates, April 1994: 38.

Bookwatch, March 1994: 9.
Locus, December 1993: 54.
Locus, October 1993: 27.
Publisher's Weekly, 18 October 1993: 67.
Library Journal, 15 October 1993: 93.
Kirkus Reviews, 1 October 1993: 1233.
Booklist, 1 September 1993: 5.

The Dolphins' Bell (in *The Chronicles of Pern: First Fall*)

Bookwatch, March 1994: 9.
Locus, January 1994: 44.

The Dolphins of Pern

Booklist, 15 September 1994: 118, 121.
Library Journal, 15 September 1994: 94.
Kirkus Reviews, 1 August 1994: 1031.

Dragondrums

Booklist, January 1986: 360.
English Journal, October 1980: 74.
Language Arts, February 1980: 189.
Analog, January 1980: 167.
Catholic Library World, December 1979: 234.
Journal of Reading, December 1979: 281.
English Journal, November 1979: 93.
Center for Children's Books Bulletin, July 1979: 195.
Horn Book Magazine, June 1979: 310.
Booklist, 1 June 1979: 1492.
School Library Journal, May 1979: 64.
Teacher, May 1979: 113.
Kirkus Reviews, 15 April 1979: 456.
Children's Book Review Service, Spring 1979: 119.

Dragonquest

Locus, October 1989: 49.
English Journal, November 1984: 89.
English Journal, October 1980: 74.
School Library Journal, May 1979: 94.
English Journal, October 1977: 93.
Times Literary Supplement, 9 November 1973: 1377.
Publisher's Weekly, 12 April 1971: 85.

The Dragonriders of Pern

Best Sellers, August 1975: 148.

Dragonsdawn

Booklist, 15 December 1990: 866.
Locus, October 1989: 49.
Publisher's Weekly, 28 July 1989: 216.
Voice of Youth Advocates, April 1989: 44.
Wilson Library Bulletin, February 1989: 94.
New York Times Book Review, 8 January 1989: 31.
Library Journal, 15 October 1988: 105.
Publisher's Weekly, 16 September 1988: 69.
Kirkus Reviews, 15 September 1988: 1366.
Booklist, 1 September 1988: 4.

Dragonsinger

Booklist, 15 October 1986: 360.
English Journal, November 1984: 89.
English Journal, October 1980: 74.
Catholic Library World, November 1977: 189.
Language Arts, October 1977: 807.
School Library Journal, September 1977: 132.
Curriculum Review, August 1977: 206.
Horn Book Magazine, June 1977: 320.
Center for Children's Books. Bulletin, May 1977: 146.

Wilson Library Bulletin, May 1977: 769.
Booklist, 1 April 1977: 1170.
Kirkus Reviews, 1 March 1977: 229.

Dragonsong

Book World (*Washington Post*), 5 November 1989: 27.
Booklist, 1 September 1987: 79.
Learning, May 1987: 47.
Booklist, 15 October 1986: 360.
English Journal, November 1984: 89.
English Journal, October 1980: 74.
English Journal, October 1977: 93.
Language Arts, September 1976: 702.
Best Sellers, August 1976: 152.
Horn Book Magazine, August 1976: 406.
Babbling Bookworm, July 1976: 4.
Center for Children's Books. Bulletin, July 1976: 177.
Booklist, 1 May 1976: 1266.
School Library Journal, April 1976: 91.
Kirkus Reviews, 1 April 1976: 391.
Publisher's Weekly, 22 March 1976: 46.

The Girl Who Heard Dragons

Locus, June 1994: 58.
Locus, May 1994: 31.
Library Journal, 15 May 1994: 103.
Kirkus Reviews, 15 May 1994: 349.
Publisher's Weekly, 9 May 1994: 68.
Booklist, 15 March 1994: 1301.

Moreta: Dragonlady of Pern

Science Fiction Chronicle, July 1993: 30.
Locus, October 1989: 49.
Kliatt Young Adult Paperback Book Guide, Winter 1985: 22.
Harper's Magazine, October 1985: 66.
Publisher's Weekly, September 1984: 95.

Analog, August 1984: 167.
Fantasy Review, August 1984: 17.
Voice of Youth Advocates, April 1984: 38.
Book Report, March 1984: 34.
School Library Journal, February 1984: 87.
Fantasy Review, January 1984: 47.
Los Angeles Times Book Review, 29 January 1984: 8.
New York Times Book Review, 8 January 1984: 18.
Publisher's Weekly, 23 September 1983: 64.
Booklist, 15 September 1983: 114.

Nerilka's Story

Locus, October 1989: 49.
Book Report, September 1987: 46.
Analog, December 1986: 177.
School Library Journal, May 1986: 114.
Booklist, 1 March 1986: 914.
Publisher's Weekly, 31 January 1986: 366.

Nerilka's Story & The Coelura

Science Fiction Chronicle, October 1987: 27.

The Renegades of Pern

Voice of Youth Advocates, April 1991: 73.
Kliatt Young Adult Paperback Book Guide, January 1991: 23.
Locus, October 1990: 52.
Locus, July 1990: 54.
Voice of Youth Advocates, April 1990: 39.
West Coast Review of Booklist, #3 1990: 34.
Locus, October 1989: 23.
Library Journal, 15 October 1989: 105.
Publisher's Weekly, 6 October 1989: 84.
Booklist, 15 September 1989: 114.
Kirkus Reviews, 15 September 1989: 1368.

Rescue Run (in *The Chronicles of Pern: First Fall*)

Locus, February 1992: 53.
Locus, October 1991: 50.

The White Dragon

Locus, October 1989: 49.
English Journal, November 1984: 89.
English Journal, October 1980: 74.
English Journal, December 1979: 74.
Ms., July 1979: 30.
Publisher's Weekly, 5 March 1979: 104.
School Library Journal, October 1978: 162.
Booklist, 1 September 1978: 39.
Library Journal, 1 June 1978: 1201.
Publisher's Weekly, 24 April 1978: 81.
Kirkus Reviews, 1 April 1978: 397.

CHAPTER 5

THE BRAIN SHIP SERIES

The City Who Fought (*The Ship Who Fought*)

Locus, August 1994: 55.
Wilson Library Bulletin, November 1993: 90.
Science Fiction Chronicle, September 1993: 34.
Voice of Youth Advocates, August 1993: 167.
Bookwatch, June 1993: 2.
Science Fiction Chronicle, June 1993: 33.
Locus, April 1993: 29.
Booklist, 1 April 1993: 1416, 1420.
Publisher's Weekly, 1 March 1993: 44.

Partnership

Voice of Youth Advocates, August 1992: 176.
Locus, February 1992: 29.

The Ship Who Sang

English Journal, November 1984: 89.
Village Voice Literary Supplement, April 1984: 19.
Magazine of Fantasy and Science Fiction, July 1970: 76.
Top of the News, June 1970: 428.
Library Journal, 15 May 1970: 1913.
Library Journal, 15 February 1970: 793.
Kirkus Reviews, 15 October 1969: 1131.
Library Journal, 1 October 1969: 3468.
Kirkus Reviews, 15 September 1969: 1033.
Publisher's Weekly, 15 September 1969: 61.

The Ship Who Searched

Locus, April 1994: 49.
Science Fiction Chronicle, September 1993: 34.
Locus, January 1993: 47.
Voice of Youth Advocates, December 1992: 293.
Kliatt Young Adult Paperback Book Guide, November 1992: 16.
Locus, September 1992: 61.

THE CRYSTAL SINGER SERIES

Crystal Line

Analog, September 1993: 160.
Kliatt Young Adult Paperback Book Guide, September 1993: 20.
Voice of Youth Advocates, 1993: 103.
School Library Journal, March 1993: 234.
Bookwatch, February 1993: 1.

Locus, November 1992: 55.
Library Journal, 15 October 1992: 104.
Booklist, October 1992: 242, 247.
Locus, September 1992: 33.
Publisher's Weekly, 28 September 1992: 68.
Kirkus Reviews, 1 September 1992: 1094.

The Crystal Singer

Fantasy Review, January 1986: 23.
English Journal, November 1984: 89.
Analog, July 1983: 100.
Voice of Youth Advocates, February 1983: 45.
Journal of Reading, November 1982: 184.
School Library Journal, November 1982: 106.
Christian Science Monitor, 29 September 1982: 15.
Los Angeles Times Book Review, 12 September 1982.
Library Journal, August 1982: 1487.
Science Fiction Review, August 1982: 24.
New York Times Book Review, 29 August 1982: 10.
Booklist, July 1982: 1394.
Science Fiction and Fantasy Book Review, July 1982: 29.
Publisher's Weekly, 25 June 1982: 116.

Killashandra

Locus, January 1991: 75.
Publisher's Weekly, November 1986: 67.
Analog, August 1986: 175.
Fantasy Review, February 1986: 23.
School Library Journal, February 1986: 103.
Library Journal, December 1985: 129.
Publisher's Weekly, 25 October 1985: 61.
Booklist, 15 October 1985: 290.
Kirkus Reviews, 15 October 1985: 1105.

CHAPTER 6

THE ROWAN SERIES

Damia

Kliatt Young Adult Paperback Book Guide, May 1993: 16.
School Library Journal, December 1992: 25, 148.
Voice of Youth Advocates, December 1992: 293.
Locus, August 1992: 54.
Publisher's Weekly, 4 May 1992: 45.
Kirkus Reviews, 1 May 1992: 577.
Locus, April 1992: 33.
Library Journal, 15 April 1992: 125.
Booklist, 1 April 1992: 1412, 1413.

Damia's Children

Kliatt Young Adult Paperback Book Guide, July 1994: 16.
School Library Journal, November 1993: 150.
Locus, February 1993: 31.
Library Journal, December 1992: 191.
Booklist, 1 December 1992: 634.
Publisher's Weekly, 23 November 1992: 56.
Kirkus Reviews, 15 November 1992: 1411.

Get Off the Unicorn

Wilson Library Bulletin, October 1977: 177.
Kliatt Young Adult Paperback Book Guide, Fall 1977: 11.
Library Journal, August 1977: 1682.
Publisher's Weekly, 2 May 1977: 67.

Lyon's Pride

New Advocate, Fall 1994: 297.
School Library Journal, September 1994: 256.

Locus, May 1994: 297.
Locus, April 1994: 49.
Locus, February 1994: 33.
Publisher's Weekly, 3 January 1994: 76.
Booklist, 1 January 1994: 788.
Kirkus Reviews, 1 January 1994: 24.

Pegasus in Flight

Voice of Youth Advocates, April 1992: 17.
Booklist, 15 March 1992: 1364.
Locus, December 1991: 54.
School Library Journal, December 1991: 35.
Locus, April 1991: 43.
School Library Journal, April 1991: 154.
Locus, February 1991: 38.
Science Fiction Chronicle, February 1991: 43.
Library Journal, December 1990: 167.
Locus, December 1990: 54.
Locus, November 1990: 27.
Booklist, 1 November 1990: 483.
Kirkus Reviews, 1 November 1990: 1503.
Publisher's Weekly, 12 October 1990: 49.

To Ride Pegasus

Voice of Youth Advocates, April 1992: 17.
Locus, December 1991: 54.
Voice of Youth Advocates, June 1991: 111.
Locus, December 1990: 54.
Times Literary Supplement, 14 March 1975: 284.
Observer, 23 February 1975: 28.

The Rowan

Voice of Youth Advocates, April 1992: 17.
Wilson Library Bulletin, November 1991: S12.
Locus, October 1991: 50.
Publisher's Weekly, 2 August 1991: 70.

Wilson Library Bulletin, May 1991: 129.
Analog, March 1991: 179.
Locus, February 1991: 38, 39.
School Library Journal, February 1991: 104.
Locus, December 1990: 54.
Locus, September 1990: 60.
Quill & Quire, September 1990: 64.
Locus, August 1990: 25.
Booklist, July 1990: 2042.
Kirkus Reviews, 15 July 1990: 971.
Publisher's Weekly, 29 June 1990: 89.

Wings of Pegasus (*Pegasus in Flight* and *To Ride Pegasus*)

Locus, July 1991: 47.

CHAPTER 7

PLANET PIRATE SERIES

Death of Sleep

Locus, February 1991: 39.
Locus, December 1990: 54.
School Library Journal, December 1990: 135.
Voice of Youth Advocates, December 1990: 300.
Locus, August 1990: 29, 48.
Booklist, July 1990: 2077.

Dinosaur Planet

Kliatt Young Adult Paperback Book Guide, Fall 1978: 18.
Library Journal, 15 June 1978: 1295.
Publisher's Weekly, 8 May 1978: 73.

Dinosaur Planet Survivors

Analog, May 1985: 135.
Fantasy Review, April 1985: 29.
Voice of Youth Advocates, April 1985: 56.
Booklist, 15 January 1985: 688.
Publisher's Weekly, 28 September 1984: 110.

Generation Warriors

Bookwatch, April 1994: 11.
Wilson Library Bulletin, February 1992: 90.
Voice of Youth Advocates, August 1991: 49.
Locus, June 1991: 49.
Kliatt Young Adult Paperback Book Guide, April 1991: 20.
Locus, April 1991: 27, 43.
Booklist, 15 March 1991: 1458.

The Planet Pirates

Voice of Youth Advocates, February 1994: 383.
Kliatt Young Adult Paperback Book Guide, January 1994: 16.
Locus, November 1993: 50.

Sassinak

Locus, February 1991: 39.
Wilson Library Bulletin, December 1990: 129.
Kliatt Young Adult Paperback Book Guide, September 1990: 22.
Locus, September 1990: 60.
Locus, August 1990: 48.
Voice of Youth Advocates, August 1990: 168.
Locus, April 1990: 25, 37.
Booklist, 1 March 1990: 1268.
Publisher's Weekly, 9 February 1990: 56.

CHAPTER 8

RESTOREE

English Journal, November 1984: 89.
Publisher's Weekly, 21 August 1967: 76.

CHAPTER 9

THE DOONA Series

Crisis on Doona

Voice of Youth Advocates, June 1992: 112.
Locus, February 1992: 29.
Publisher's Weekly, 10 February 1992: 77.

Decision at Doona

Books & Bookmen, July 1970: 43.
Publisher's Weekly, 17 March 1969: 58.

Treaty at Doona (Treaty Planet)

Locus, June 1994: 35.
Books, January 1994: 17.

CHAPTER 10

THE POWERS SERIES

Power Lines

Locus, August 1994: 55.
Locus, June 1994: 35.
Publisher's Weekly, 23 May 1994: 81.
Library Journal, 15 May 1994: 103.
Kirkus Reviews, 1 May 1994: 595.
Booklist, 1 April 1994: 1404.

Powers That Be

Locus, July 1994: 59.
Analog, April 1994: 168.
Voice of Youth Advocates, April 1994: 19.
Locus, February 1994: 58.
School Library Journal, January 1994: 145.
Bookwatch, December 1993: 6.
Wilson Library Bulletin, November 1993: 90.
Locus, August 1993: 46.
Science Fiction Chronicle, July 1993: 32.
Locus, May 1993: 33.
Publisher's Weekly, 17 May 1993: 70.
Library Journal, 15 May 1993: 99.
Booklist, 15 April 1993: 1470.
Kirkus Reviews, 15 April 1993: 494.

The Coelura

Locus, November 1989: 56.
Voice of Youth Advocates, April 1988: 40.
Publisher's Weekly, 27 November 1987: 71.
Science Fiction and Fantasy Book Review, July 1983: 39.
Library Journal, 15 June 1983: 1278.
Publisher's Weekly, 13 May 1983: 39.
Kliatt Young Adult Paperback Book Guide, 15 April 1983.

Index

About the Author

ROBIN ROBERTS is Associate Professor of English and Women's and Gender Studies at Louisiana State University. She is the author of *A New Species: Gender and Science in Science Fiction* (1993), *Ladies First: Feminist Music Videos* (forthcoming), and numerous articles on science fiction.

Recent Titles in
Critical Companions to Popular Contemporary Writers
Kathleen Gregory Klein, Series Editor

Mary Higgins Clark: A Critical Companion
Linda C. Pelzer

Michael Crichton: A Critical Companion
Elizabeth A. Trembley

V. C. Andrews: A Critical Companion
E. D. Huntley